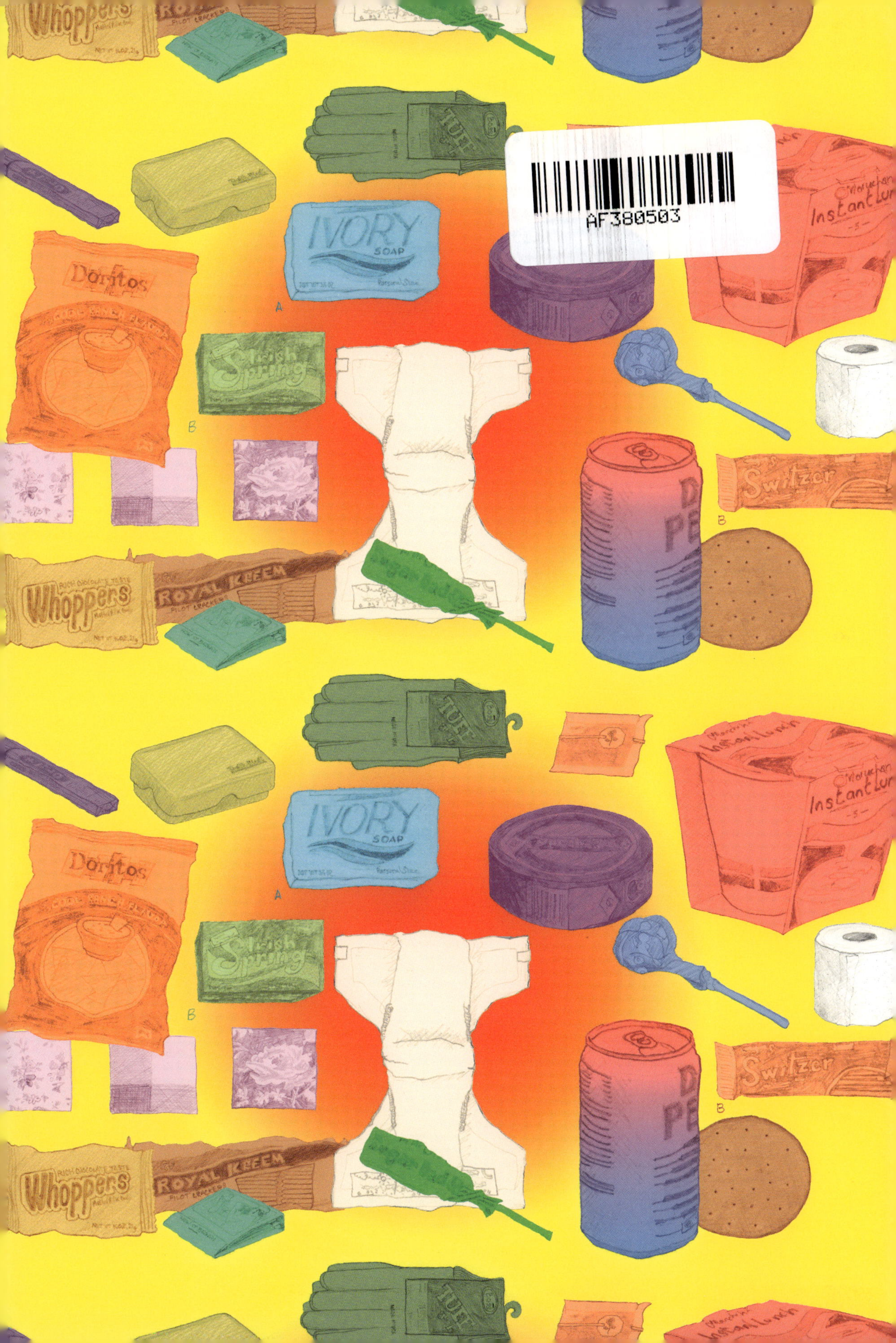

Whoppers
Doritos
IVORY SOAP
Irish Spring
ROYAL KREEM
PILOT CRACKERS
Whoppers
Switzer
Instant Lum
TUFF

JEFFREY GIBSON: BEYOND THE HORIZON

EDITED BY ABIGAIL WINOGRAD AND JEFFREY GIBSON

SMART MUSEUM OF ART
THE UNIVERSITY OF CHICAGO

EDITOR'S NOTE:

Throughout this publication, the editors have chosen to use the term Indigenous, with a capital I, rather than Native American, to refer to the original inhabitants of the United States. Some authors prefer the term Native American as an acknowledgment of the specificity of their work with the Indigenous peoples of the United States of America. We recognize that authors have nuanced approaches to the expression of identity through language and respect the preference to use Native American as a descriptor.

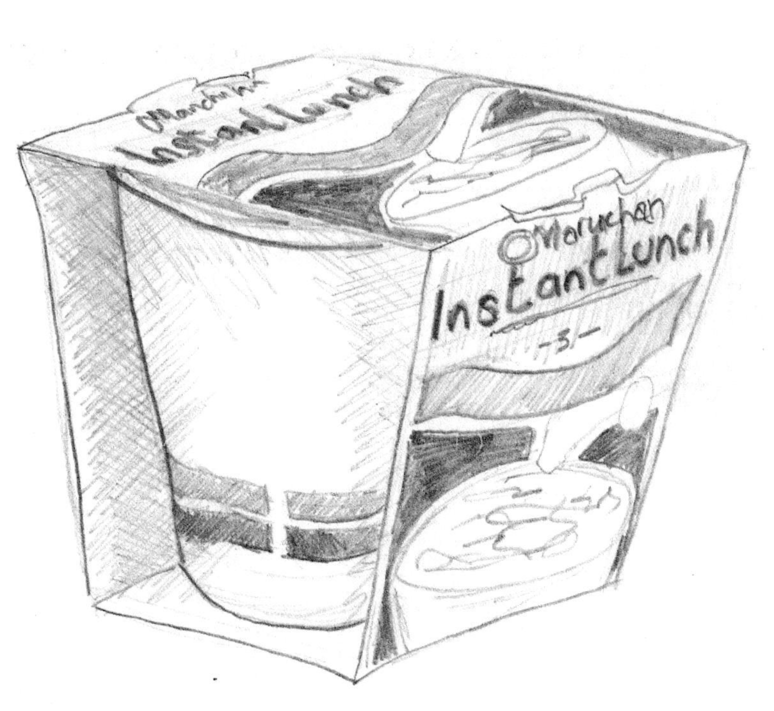
Maruchan
Instant Lunch
Maruchan
Instant Lunch
-3.-

FIELD MUSEUM OF NATURAL HISTORY—ETHNOLOGY 2-2

181110

Field No.

–

Neg. No.

Acc. 3784

Provenience: Toksook Bay, Nelson Is., Alaska

People or Culture: Yupik Eskimo

Object: "instant lunch"

Material: –

Description: "Maruchan" oriental noodles with vegetables and egg, beef flavor (1 container - 2.25 oz.)
Used as gift in seal party.

Dimensions: –
(in cm.)

Collection: Dr. Ann Fienup-Riordan

5

Over the last three decades, Jeffrey Gibson's multidisciplinary practice has brilliantly blended Indigenous forms and materials with those of modern and contemporary Western art to create a new visual vocabulary. Gibson's work is deeply rooted in the historical canon, and from this vantage point he redresses the absence of Indigenous peoples—their visual cultures and personhood—from the history of Western art. He deftly incorporates references to popular culture, music, queer iconography, and contemporary politics into painting, video, clothing, and sculpture.

This catalogue explores a recent turning point in Gibson's practice—a foray into portraiture—prompted by the artist's participation in *Toward Common Cause: Art, Social Change, and the MacArthur Fellows Program at 40*, an intensive set of interrelated projects led by the Smart Museum of Art in collaboration with partner organizations across Chicago. In Gibson's case, that partner was the Newberry Library, and the resulting project was *Sweet Bitter Love*. This beautifully troubling, site-responsive installation reflects Gibson's research into institutional histories and collections (at and beyond the library itself). In it, Gibson has distilled years of practice into elegant and moving comments on the histories of the Americas, art, and institutions.

This book thus brings together a body of work that lives across the histories and spaces of Chicago, and it exists through the dedication and effort of many individuals.

First, a huge debt of gratitude goes to Abigail Winograd, the Smart Museum of Art's MacArthur Fellows Program Fortieth Anniversary Exhibition Curator, for conceiving this project in partnership with the artist, and for working tirelessly to bring it to life. Deep thanks are also due to Paul Durica, curator at the Newberry Library, for his willingness to open himself and his institution to Gibson's intervention.

Additionally, we would like to acknowledge the commitment and support of the entire Newberry Library staff. In particular, *Sweet Bitter Love* would not have been possible without the capable hands and minds of Rose Miron, director of the D'Arcy McNickle Center for American Indian and Indigenous Studies; Analú Lopez, Ayer

Indigenous studies librarian; and Amanda Cacich, assistant registrar and exhibition specialist. We would also like to think the team at Kavi Gupta Chicago for presenting the parallel exhibition *Beyond the Horizon* and for the gallery's support of both exhibitions and this publication.

At the Smart Museum, we would like to acknowledge the entire team who worked to bring *Toward Common Cause* as a whole and *Sweet Bitter Love* specifically to life, with great enthusiasm and earnestness. While everyone at the museum contributed to *Toward Common Cause*, particular appreciation is due to Sara Hindmarch, former head registrar; Ray Klemchuk, associate director of exhibition design and production; and Jenna Post, assistant registrar for their work on *Sweet Bitter Love*.

Heartfelt thanks also go to the contributors to this catalogue. Kathleen Ash-Milby, Christian Ayne Crouch, Dieter Roelstraete, and Abigail Winograd offer thoughtful perspectives that allow readers direct access to the artist's voice and share diverse interpretations of the works at the heart of this project. Special thanks also go to two Smart Museum colleagues: Gail Ana Gomez, who skillfully guided this publication, and intern Norman Mora Quintero, who worked diligently on image captions and credits.

Finally—and most essentially—I would like to acknowledge the artist, Jeffrey Gibson. Thank you for your dedication, your insight, and your wisdom. You created an extraordinary project that has been deeply meaningful to your collaborators and inspiring for those of us lucky enough to experience *Sweet Bitter Love* in Chicago. We are grateful for your ongoing collaboration on this generous and beautiful publication, which now will reach many others. Thank you!

Stephanie Smith
Interim Director
Smart Museum of Art, The University of Chicago

ACKNOWLEDGMENTS

I am honored to have worked with Jeffrey Gibson over the last several years to bring this exhibition and publication to fruition. My invitation to Gibson to participate in *Toward Common Cause: Art, Social Change, and the MacArthur Fellows Program at 40* and his contribution to that sprawling, multisite exhibition, *Sweet Bitter Love*, marked the beginning of an incredible journey, and I am very grateful for his willingness to embark upon it with me.

This book brings together work and ideas from two exhibitions, *Sweet Bitter Love: An Initiative of Toward Common Cause* at the Newberry Library and *Beyond the Horizon* at Kavi Gupta, Chicago. It reflects on Gibson's research and engagement with the city of Chicago, its institutions, and their relationships to Indigenous peoples, cultures, and histories.

We extend our gratitude to our partners in the development of the exhibitions and this publication. *Toward Common Cause: Art, Social Change, and the MacArthur Fellows Program at 40* was organized by the Smart Museum of Art at the University of Chicago in collaboration with exhibition, programmatic, and research partners across Chicago. It was supported by the John D. and Catherine T. MacArthur Foundation. Additional support for Gibson's participation and this publication was provided by Kavi Gupta, Chicago. Thank you to our partners at the Newberry Library, Paul Durica, Rose Miron, Analú Lopez, and Amanda Cacich. I would also like to thank the team at the Field Museum, Alaka Wali and Lauren Hancock, for their assistance.

I hope this publication offers the reader insight into Gibson's practice and provides context for these two exhibitions, as well as this important moment of development in his career. For the perspectives and wisdom offered in their contributions to this volume, I'd like to thank Kathleen Ash-Milby, Christian Ayne Crouch, and Dieter Roelstraete.

Unyimeabasi Udoh, thank you for your thoughtful and beautiful design of this volume, which captures not only both exhibitions but also the spirit of the artist's work. Thank you to the University of Chicago Press for working with us to distribute this book; we are thrilled to have this wonderful opportunity to work with you. Thank you to Norman Mora Quintero, the Smart's publications intern, who helped with image permissions and captions. And thank you to Amy Teschner, for your guidance, helpful comments, and edits as we finalized all the book text.

At the Smart Museum of Art, I want to especially thank Ray Klemchuk, associate director of design and production for exhibitions, and the Smart's preparator Derek Ernster, for the commitment and hard work they put into the exhibition, as well as Sara Hindmarch, former head registrar, for skillfully bringing this exhibition to life in Chicago. Thank you to Bill Michel and Amina Dickerson, former interim directors of the Smart Museum, for their support during the run-up to the exhibition, and Stephanie Smith, current interim director, for her support of the project. Special thanks are due to Simone Levine, former curatorial research assistant for global contemporary art, and Sarah Markowitz, curatorial intern, for their diligent research, writing, and administrative management. To Jill Sterrett and Michael Christiano, thank you for your inspiration and partnership.

To Gail Ana Gomez, the Smart Museum's exhibitions and publications manager, thank you for your grace under pressure, deft attention to detail, and collaboration. We have worked through impossible circumstances, and this project truly would not have been possible without you.

Finally, an enormous thank you to Jeffrey! Thank you for trusting me with this endeavor. It has been my honor and privilege to get to know you, to work with you, and to realize these projects together. I have learned so much.

Abigail Winograd
MacArthur Fellows Program Fortieth Anniversary
Exhibition Curator
Smart Museum of Art, The University of Chicago

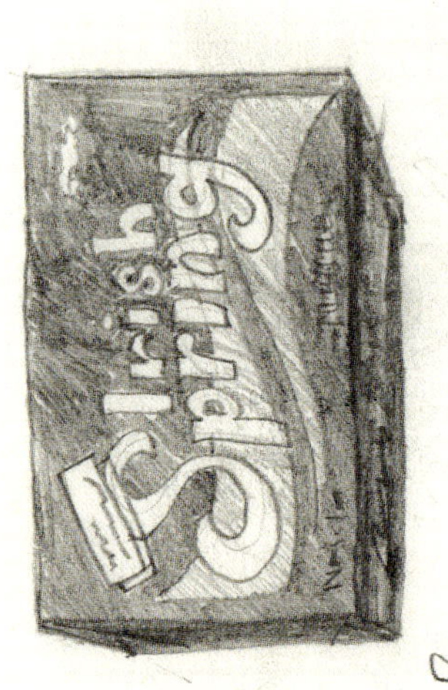
Irish Spring
B

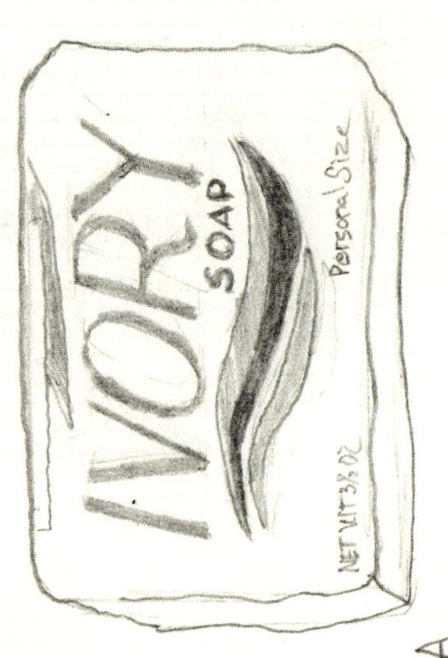
IVORY
SOAP
Personal Size
NET WT 3.5 OZ
A

FIELD MUSEUM OF NATURAL HISTORY—ETHNOLOGY 2-2?

Field No.

–

Provenience: Toksook Bay, Nelson Is., Alaska

People or Culture: Yupik Eskimo

Object: soap

Material: –

Description: A) "Ivory" (1 bar – $3\frac{1}{2}$ oz.)
B) "Irish Spring" (1 bar – 2.5 oz.)

Used as gift in seal party.

Neg. No.

Dimensions: –
(in cm.)

Acc. 3784

Collection: Dr. Ann Fienup-Riordan

11

BEADING FOR BONETA, A GIFT FOR PAUL LEE: JEFFREY GIBSON'S TESSELLATED HISTORIES

ABIGAIL WINOGRAD

Sweet, sweet bitter love
What joy you brought me
And what pain you taught me
I'm so sure I'll stay
And my magic dreams
Have lost their spell
Where there was hope
There's just an empty shell
Sweet, sweet bitter love
Why have you awakened
And then forsaken
A trusting heart like mine?

—Van McCoy, "Sweet Bitter Love,"
as sung by Roberta Flack on her album *Quiet Fire*

The juxtaposition of objects across geographical, temporal, and cultural boundaries was at the crux of *Sweet Bitter Love*—the first institutional exhibition in Chicago to present works by Chahta (Choctaw) and Tsalagihi (Cherokee) artist Jeffrey Gibson.[1] *Sweet Bitter Love* drew together four distinct sets of objects: two groups of paintings (one by Elbridge Ayer (E. A.) Burbank and the other by Gibson), accession cards from Chicago's Field Museum, and a site-specific wallpaper. The display, in the Newberry Library's Hanson Gallery, included six new portraits painted by Gibson, reimagined versions of Burbank's originals. Some of Burbank's works hung against the backdrop of a site-specific wallpaper designed by Gibson incorporating drawings from the catalogue cards.[2] The accession cards document the entrance of a cache of objects into the museum's collection in 1991. These were gifts given during an *uqiquq* (a "seal party" that celebrates a Yupik man's first seasonal catch of a bearded seal), according to the accession records. Gibson's paintings marked a significant shift in his practice as they are the artist's first foray in portraiture, a genre he has long avoided because of its links to and complicity in settler violence and colonial chauvinism.[3] In light of the baggage thus associated with portraiture, Gibson has been wary of painting people. Yet the

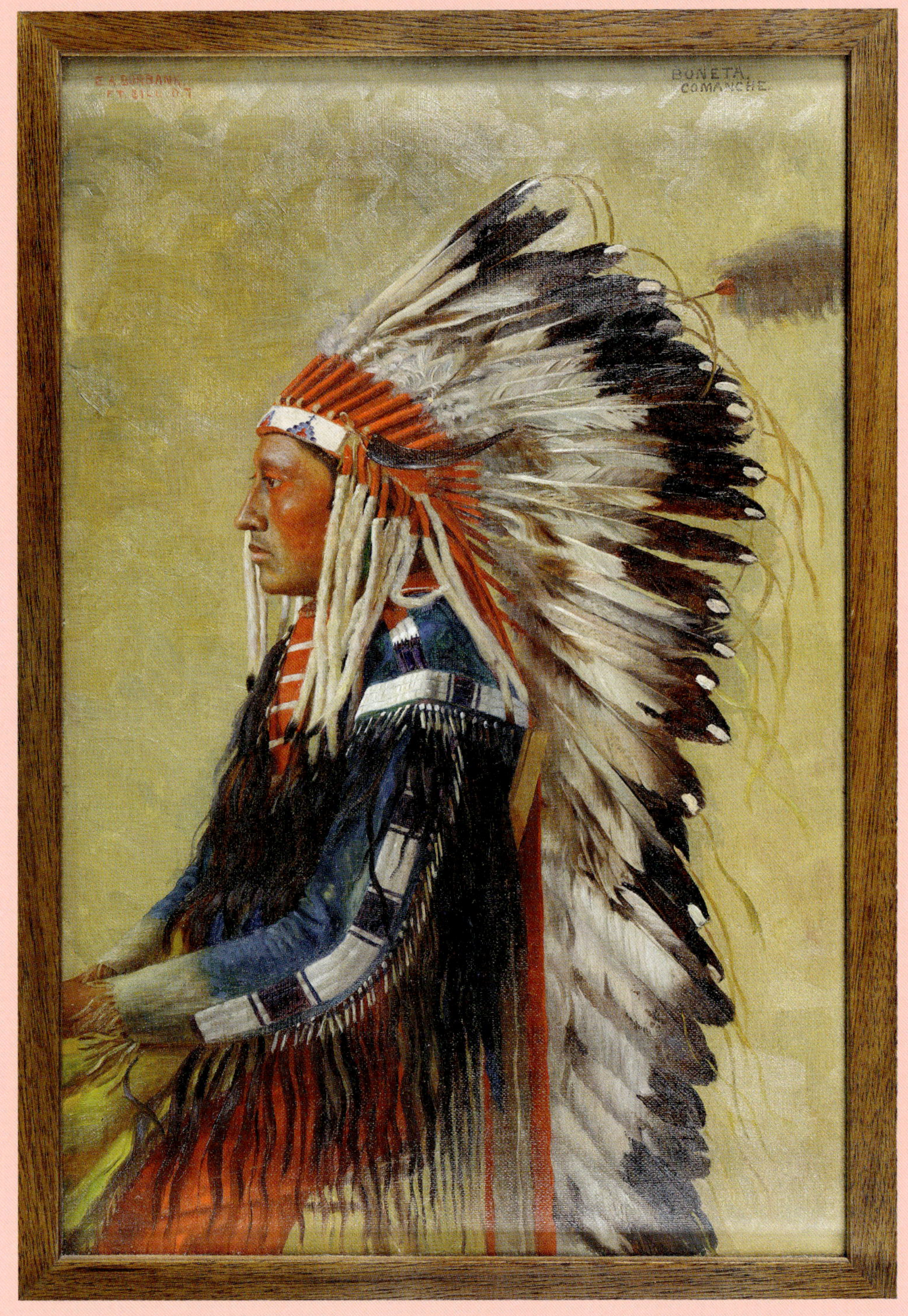

1: Elbridge Ayer Burbank, *Boneta*, Fort Sill, Oklahoma Territory, undated [1897]. Oil on canvas. 21 1/8 x 14 1/4 inches (53.7 x 36.2 cm). Newberry Library, Chicago.

opportunity to craft a rejoinder to institutional histories of complicity and neglect overwhelmed his ambivalence.

The exhibition's eponymous title came from the song sung by Roberta Flack on her 1971 album *Quiet Fire*. Evoking the pain of unrequited love, "Sweet Bitter Love" is an apt metaphor for the works in the exhibition and Gibson's complex relationship to the depiction of Indigenous peoples, the history of Indigenous portraiture, and the institutions that frequently house them. All the elements of his years of aesthetic experimentation are here: ornament, embellishment, pattern, abstraction, beading, and vibrant colors. The works continue to evince Gibson's interest in self-expression viewed through the traditions of Indigenous dress and self-representation. He continues to deploy kitsch as a form of resistance and to deconstruct the ways in which it has been used to delegitimize cultural expressions in music, dance, or art that exist outside of or challenge the mainstream. He continues to engage with the history of postwar abstraction. These paintings represent a refinement of Gibson's vision in their restrained assemblage. Despite retaining the exuberance of Gibson's oeuvre, these portraits radiate an aura of somber, elegiac nostalgia.

The Red River War, the last major conflict between the United States and the tribes of the Southern Plains, ended in 1875 with the surrender of Quanah Parker and several hundred Nʉmʉnʉʉ (Comanche) warriors at Fort Sill, Oklahoma, on June 2, 1875. There, Burbank, a turn-of-the-century American artist best known for his paintings and sketches of Indigenous people, painted *Boneta* (undated [1897], fig. 1). Burbank himself arrived at Fort Sill in 1897 at the behest of his uncle Edward E. Ayer, a prominent Chicago businessman, president of the Field Museum of Natural History, and an avid collector of books and Indigenous artifacts. Ayer sent his nephew to paint a portrait of Goyaałé (known as Geronimo), the infamous Nde (Chiricahua Apache) war chief, who was imprisoned there along with thousands of other Indigenous people, to create a record of the end of Indigenous resistance and the assimilation of the tribes into American society. Burbank stayed at Fort Sill for two months painting dozens of portraits, many of which were intended for and remain in the care of the Newberry Library.[4]

Burbank painted Boneta in profile in full regalia—eagle feather war bonnet and a beaded and fringed shirt—against a brownish-gold background. As Burbank frequently asked his subjects to wear ceremonial clothing, we cannot know if this is how Boneta wanted to be seen. He stares, impassive and motionless, into the distance. The ways in which Burbank denied the personhood and internal life of his sitters are most evident when contrasted with Burbank's portrait of his Uncle Ayer from the same year (*Edward Everett Ayer*, 1897, fig. 2). Ayer sits in a rocking chair surrounded by his collection of books and objects. He stares directly at the viewer, his finger in a volume, head knowingly tilted to one side. Burbank provides Boneta with no such comforts or evidence of individuality.

From 1750 to 1850, the Nʉmunʉʉ Nation ruled a 240,000-square-mile territory that stretched across the present-day North American Southwest. Comanchería, as it was dubbed by the Spanish, was governed by a decentralized but economically and socially complex political system that traded with, drew tribute, and extracted labor from surrounding Indigenous and colonial entities alike. The Nʉmunʉʉ language, a Shoshone dialect, became the lingua franca for tribes in the area. After the Spanish brought horses to the region, the tribe used the resource to become an elite military power. The Nʉmunʉʉ's prowess in battle inspired such fear in Euro-American colonists that they can be credited with effectively halting, if not pushing back, the seemingly endless march of westward expansion. Indeed, the Spanish were so wary of the ferocity and skill of Nʉmunʉʉ warriors that they likewise ended their northward push a century earlier, and they strategically deployed Texas and its settlers as a buffer to protect themselves from the financial and human losses incurred by confronting the Nʉmunʉʉ head-on. It is not an exaggeration to state that the Nʉmunʉʉ played a prominent and decisive role in the transatlantic colonial story of the Americas.[5] The fact that this reality is so little known is at least partially due to its subversion of conventional historical narratives that portray Indigenous people as isolated, disempowered victims who were laid low by sickness, forcibly displaced by settlers, and overwhelmed by the power of the US military. Recent scholarship describes a more nuanced narrative. US

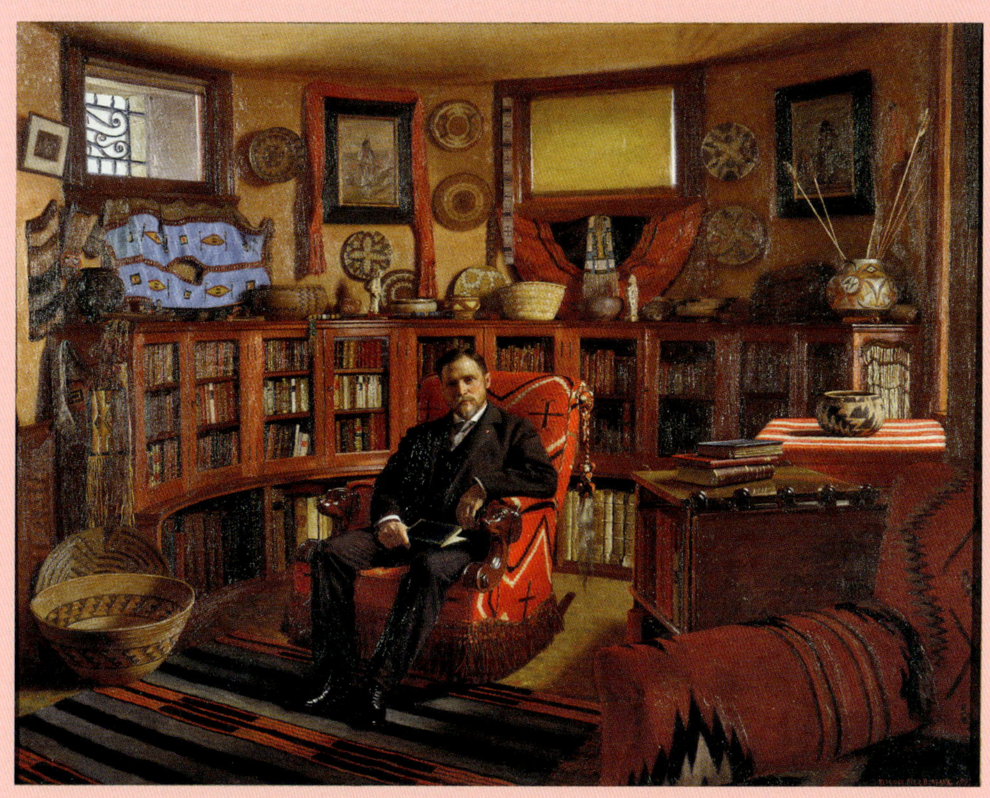

2: Elbridge Ayer Burbank, *Edward Everett Ayer*, 1897. Oil on canvas. 24 ½ x 31 ½ inches (62.2 x 80 cm). Newberry Library, Chicago.

settler colonialism was undoubtedly devastating to Indigenous communities, but the *Nʉmunʉʉ* and other Indigenous peoples played an active role in thwarting North American and European imperial intentions, thereby contributing to the geography, history, and culture of the United States, Europe, and the rest of the Americas. None of this proud history, all part of Boneta's story, can be inferred from Burbank's work. In fact, Burbank's portraits were an integral part of a larger anthropological and historical enterprise that anonymized Indigenous people, stripping them of their traditional homelands, objects, and expressions.

The problem with Burbank's paintings and their ilk is their enduring, seemingly unshakeable, power to efface the humanity, history, and culture of Indigenous people. As the Anglo-American artists of the nineteenth and early-twentieth century painted Indigenous portraits, they muted the emotions of their sitters, flattened history, erased complexity, and actively perpetuated the pervasive and pernicious lie that the Indigenous peoples of North America and their multifaceted, multiethnic traditions were disappearing.[6] Burbank's work was complicit in the stereotypical and ubiquitous two-dimensional version of US history all around us. Nʉmunʉʉ curator Paul Chaat Smith has described the peculiar place of Indigenous imagery within the visual culture of the United States thusly:

> Even as they [the colonists] plotted their removal, they idealized the hell out of the Indigenous.... As the decades rolled along, Indian imagery became not just present but ubiquitous. Airlines, insurance companies, brake fluid, whisky, cigarettes, software, hotels, motorcycles, cruise missiles, sports cars, attack helicopters, bottled water, atomic-bomb tests, baking powder, fruit boxes, and a third of the states and streets in every town and city in the country—we were used as symbols for every manner of product, and, eventually, a symbol of the country itself.... From the very beginning, then, Indians were both everywhere and nowhere. These Indians that are the visual wallpaper of American life are, of course, mostly generic and imaginary. They are around us constantly yet calibrated to never draw very much attention.

It is a phenomenon so utterly singular, yet so brilliantly normalized that we rarely think anything of it. It masks its power in kitsch, always whispering to us "nothing to see here," from our pantries and highways and stadiums and the names of the land and cities and towns.[7]

Why do these paintings still wield such power? Why, after more than a century has passed, must we continue to refute Burbank's claims to historical accuracy? How do institutions continue to reinforce those claims and how can we deconstruct them?

Gibson's relationship to Chicago and its cultural institutions is substantial. He graduated from the School of the Art Institute in 1995 and worked at the Field Museum while he was a student. His job was to prepare for and assist tribal delegations coming to the Field to visit their cultural patrimony. These visits began following the passage of the Native American Graves Protection and Repatriation Act (NAGPRA) in 1990.[8] Gibson's experience at the Field Museum decisively molded his understanding of museums and their relationship to Indigenous American culture and communities. In his encounters with tribal delegations, Gibson occupied a middle space: a citizen of the Mississippi Band of Chahta, he was an outsider to the culture of the tribal representatives he met, yet keenly felt the weight of honoring their connections to sacred objects. He experienced the multiethnic fabric of Indigenous America, as well as the scope and scale of the forced internal migration of Indigenous communities. He saw firsthand how institutions perpetuate the fetishization of objects by placing all forms of knowledge in relation to the dominant Euro-American narrative. This experience thus gave Gibson profound insight into how institutions shape what we are, how we see, and our relationship to the past. It was during his time at the Field Museum that Gibson first encountered the uqiquq gifts documented in the accession cards included in *Sweet Bitter Love* (fig. 3). The discussion surrounding this acquisition—whether a collecting institution should be accessioning objects that could be purchased at a grocery store, such as diapers, Doritos, and SKOL—had a tremendous influence on how Gibson

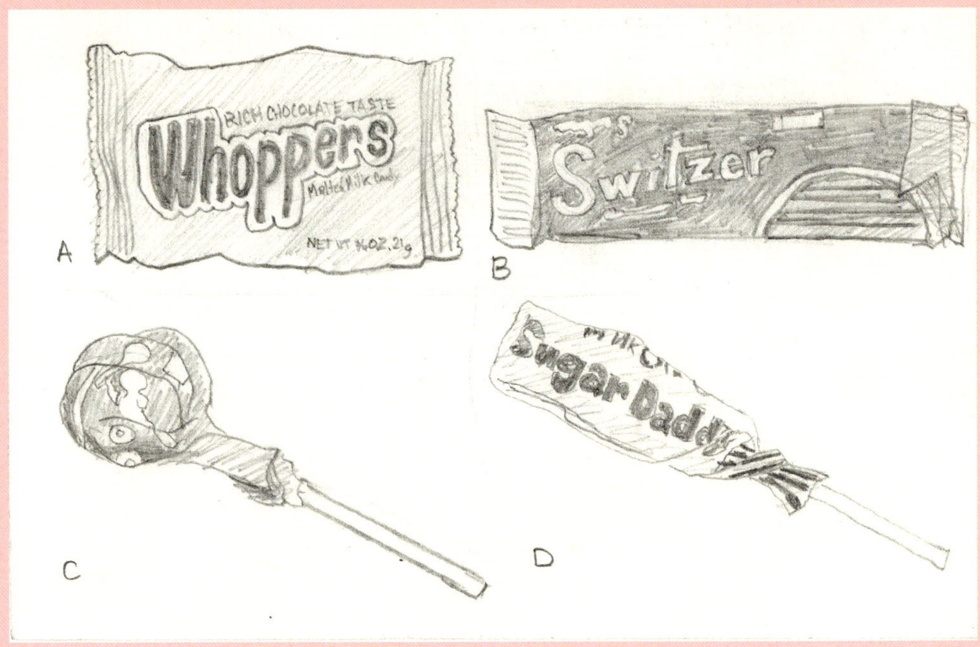

3: Field Museum Catalogue Card (verso), Nelson Island Seal Party Collection, Accession 3784, *Candy*, 1990. Cat. No. 181111. The Field Museum, Chicago.

views anthropological museums, their collecting policies, and the way in which institutions fashion our (mis)understandings of contemporary Indigenous communities. It reinforced his conviction that the culture at large remains invested in the myth of Indigenous America created by artists like Burbank—a history enshrined in archival and institutional collections, one that continues to obscure the lived experience of Indigenous communities.

The decision to paint these portraits, *Boneta, Comanche*; *Chief Pretty Eagle*; *Chief Black Coyote*; *Christian Naiche*; *Pahl Lee*; and *White Swan* (all 2021), stems from Gibson's antipathy for Burbank's paintings. What would it mean to repaint Boneta? In Gibson's version, the Comanche warrior's figure appears five times nestled into a field of orange triangles, circles, and squares (fig. 4). In the middle left, the orange gives way to shades of green and the details of Boneta's features—high cheekbones, full lips, strong nose, and soft eyes—emerge. We see the beaded band of his war bonnet; its fur side hangings frame his face. A hand-beaded frame of green, yellow, red, and black encloses his visage. Outside the frame the geometric patterning of the image derives from the portrait; the horizontal band of his bonnet appears as a motif repeated in the beaded belt at the picture's top left and the beaded collar at its bottom. Boneta's nose has a sharp angle that echoes in the linear and circular tessellations of right triangles. Three circles frame found objects, a beaded barrette, a novelty game piece—made in Japan and depicting a young boy with a red headband with a feather—and a repoussé bangle portraying an elderly man with braids and feathers in his hair.[9] The resultant combination of portraiture and abstraction allows Gibson to open new vistas, to incorporate the sitter into a larger story of both the history and art of the United States.

In *Boneta, Comanche*, Gibson, as in all the paintings in *Sweet Bitter Love*, juxtaposes his own beading with beaded objects purchased from websites and estate and garage sales. Gibson does not know the precise dates of execution for these pieces of handwork, though he can guess when they were made. Gibson does not know their makers, though they span generations in much the same manner, as the practice has been passed down through families. The beadwork itself represents a complicated, often painful, history of survival and adaptation. Gibson is interested in the hybridity, aesthetic ingenuity, and commercial necessity that they represent. Aside from their historical indexicality, each handmade piece creates a physical, human connection to the maker, the tradition, and the past. Anyone who has watched an episode of *Antiques Roadshow* will have heard an appraiser dismiss an Indigenous artifact made for the tourist trade as a negative, a reason to diminish its resale price. Gibson places a value on these objects that refutes the market's preference for objects with a veneer of authenticity, those with a connection to a mythic past rather than the layered reality we all presently inhabit.

 Sweet Bitter Love was a meditation on context. The obvious differences between Burbank's *Boneta* and Gibson's *Boneta, Comanche* are an integral part of the latter's critical endeavor—a probing exercise in the art of recontextualization, both from within and without the art-historical mainstream, as well as a reconsideration of the hegemonic history of white America. The beaded handbag, a jewel-like gift for the beautiful *Pahl Lee*, the "I'm Entitled" button at the center of *Christian Naiche*, and the inverted United States flag below Chief Pretty Eagle offer a refutation to the history of Indigenous portraiture and gestures of care to the sitters. In this act of rebuttal, Gibson's project is clearly aligned with the tradition of Institutional Critique, which may well be conceptual art's most enduring (and certainly most topical) legacy. The meaning of *Sweet Bitter Love* unfolded along the fissures that separate insiders from outsiders, centers from peripheries, victors from victims, mainstreams from margins, arts from crafts. And it is clear from our making sense of the complexities and riches of Gibson's four-part installation that the artist is securely and confidently inside the machine of art—the perfect vantage point from which to think history anew.

In a fitting epilogue to *Sweet Bitter Love*, Gibson included *Chief Pretty Eagle, Christian Naiche, Pahl Lee, Boneta, White Swan,* and *Chief Black Coyote* in an exhibition titled *Beyond the Horizon* at Kavi Gupta in October of 2021. In the white cube of the gallery likewise transformed by Gibson's wallpaper, the six works were no longer behind glass,

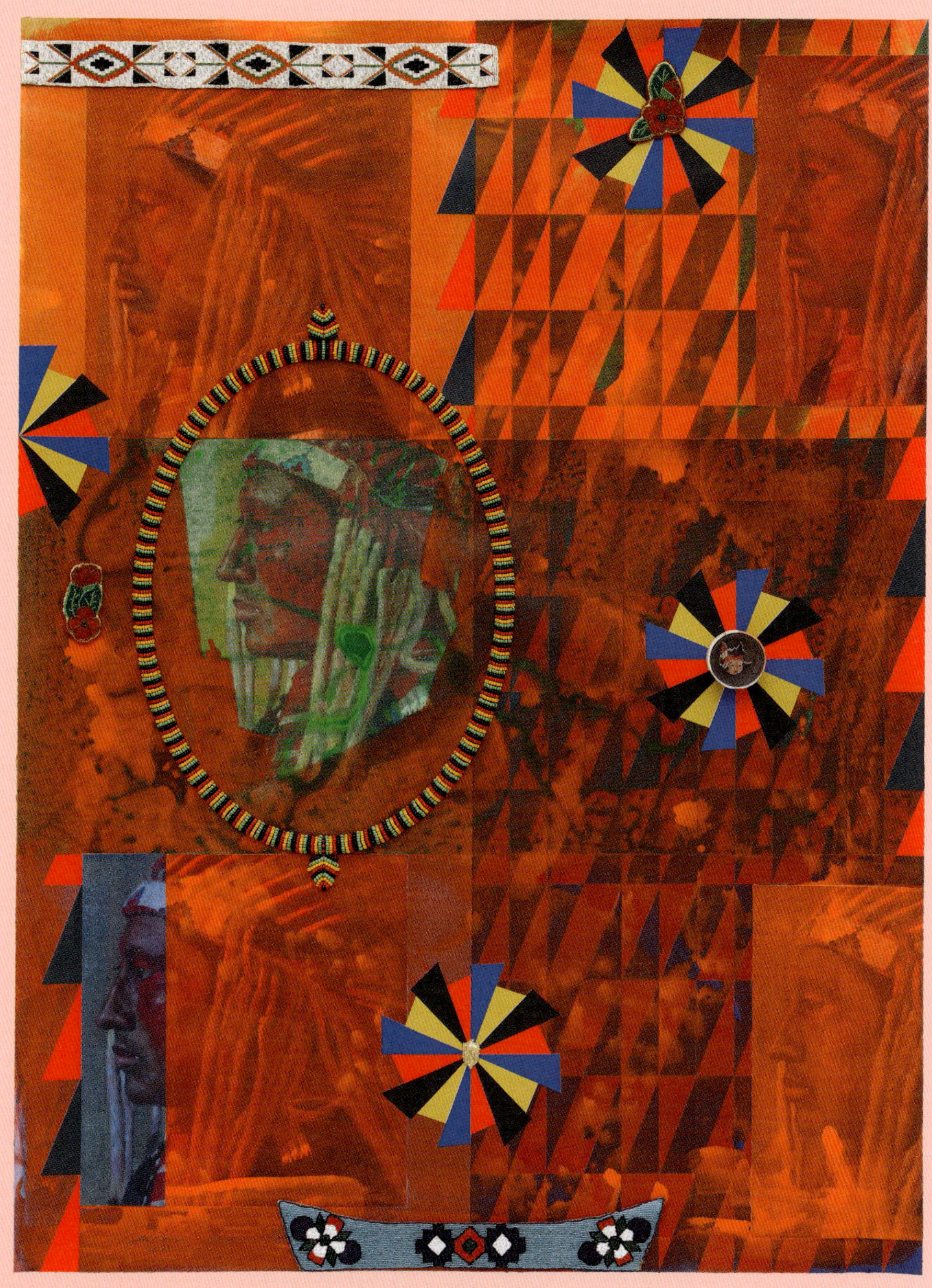

4: Jeffrey Gibson, *Boneta, Comanche*, 2021. Cotton rag paper, archival pigment print, glass beads, nylon thread, vintage beaded belt (glass beads, suede, and cotton thread), vintage beaded barrettes (glass beads, suede, polyester, and thread), vintage ring toss game from Japan (print, cardboard, and clear plastic), brass repoussé, vintage papers, glass beads, urethane, and acrylic paint. 60 1/2 × 44 inches (153.7 × 111.8 cm). Collection of Mitchell and Debbie Rechler.

which allowed a proper viewing of their layers and textures (fig. 5). They appeared even more vibrant, more complex, and more audacious. It was as though they had been finally freed from their entombment. I was overwhelmed to see them this way. It was an encounter that only reinforced the power of context in shaping what and how we see. As this was the question at the center of this new body of work, both of these exhibitions are included in this volume as a document of the posthumous travels of Chief Pretty Eagle, Christian Naiche, Pahl Lee, Boneta, White Swan, and Chief Black Coyote.

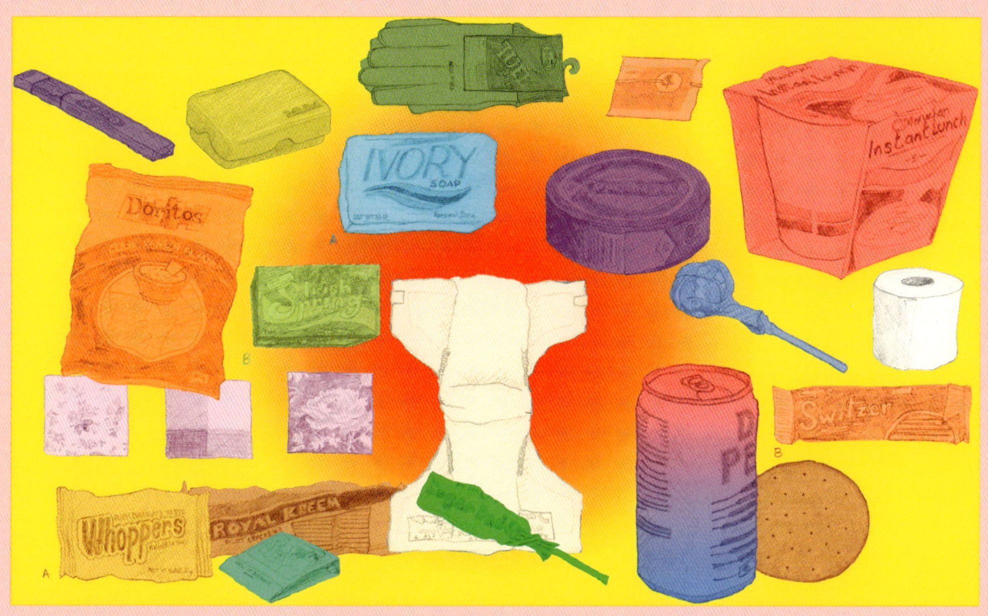

5: Jeffrey Gibson, *Acc. 3784*, 2021. Digitally printed wallpaper on vinyl. Dimensions variable. Courtesy of Jeffrey Gibson.

NOTES

1   *Sweet Bitter Love* was presented at the Newberry Library in Chicago from May 28 to September 18, 2021, as part of *Toward Common Cause: Art, Social Change, and the MacArthur Fellows Program at 40. Toward Common Cause* was a multisite exhibition organized by the Smart Museum of Art at the University of Chicago in collaboration with more than two dozen exhibition, programmatic, and research partners across the city of Chicago throughout 2021.

2   Gibson selected six works from the Newberry's holdings of Burbank's paintings. However, not all the works could be displayed due to conservation concerns. For Gibson, this was symptomatic of larger questions of respect, or lack thereof, typically shown by collecting institutions to Indigenous materials, and in this instance to the sitters and their descendants. This situation drove Gibson's decision to persist in re-creating images by Burbank that could not face their doppelgangers. The purpose of the portraits was to evince the humanity and complexity of the individuals. For example, the hand-beaded frames are an act of care, a gesture of love. In the end, it was not important that there be a one-to-one correlation with the portraits on either side of the gallery; they are in the building and therefore they are present

3   Depictions of the Indigenous peoples of the Americas made by Europeans first appeared in the late sixteenth century. The original images were a kind of reportage accompanying the accounts of the first encounters with Indigenous communities and descriptions of the lands encountered across the Atlantic. They were made for European audiences and positioned Indigenous Americans as the barbarous other in contrast to European civilization. As more delegations of Indigenous people voyaged across the Atlantic to the courts of England, France, and Spain, their likenesses were recorded by artists like Sir Joshua Reynolds. In the eighteenth and nineteenth centuries, US officials frequently commissioned portraits of Indigenous leaders following the signing of treaties with the government. As the campaign to annex territories and eradicate Indigenous cultures and people legalized in the passage of President Andrew Jackson's Indian Removal Act of 1830, the desire to capture images of the "vanishing race" resulted in an abundance of images produced by the likes of George Catlin and Burbank himself. Stephanie Pratt, "George Catlin and the Representation of the North American Indian," in *George Catlin: American Indian Portraits* (London: National Portrait Gallery, 2013), 17–29.

4   For more on Burbank, see
"Burbank among the Indians:
the Politics of Patronage,"
in *Martin Padget, Indian
Country: Travels in the
American Southwest, 1840–1935*
(Albuquerque: University of
New Mexico Press, 2004),
137–68.

5   Pekka Hämäläinen, *The
Comanche Empire* (New Haven,
CT: Yale University Press), 2008.

6   Burbank's paintings follow
the works of nineteenth-
century artists, scholars,
and ethnographers who
propagated the myth that
Indigenous Americans were a
"Vanishing Race" that needed
to be preserved through
documentation. See Matt Clark,
"Image-Making: E. A. Burbank's
Portraits of Geronimo,"
Newbery Library (blog),
November 8, 2018, https://www.
newberry.org/image-making-ea-
burbanks-portraits-geronimo.

7   Paul Chaat Smith, "Indian Art
for Modern Living," in *Art for
a New Understanding: Native
Voices, 1950s to Now*, ed. Mindy
N. Besaw, Candice Hopkins,
and Manuela Well-Off-Man
(Fayetteville: University of
Arkansas Press, 2018), 92–100.

8   The federal legislation known as
NAGRPA provided a framework
for access to and the repatriation
of funerary objects, sacred
objects, and cultural patrimony.

9   The Indian Arts and Crafts
Act (IACA) was signed into
law by President George H. W.
Bush in 1990. IACA made it a
felony for an individual who
was not an enrolled member of
a federally recognized tribe to
sell or display work designated
as "Indian." The professed
goal of IACA was to prevent
the importation of "Indian"
handicrafts produced abroad.
It provided legal recourses and
penalties of up to five years of
imprisonment or a $250,000 fine
for individuals or institutions
convicted of falsely labeling
objects. Among the bill's myriad
unintended consequences are
museum closures such as the
Museum of the Five Civilized
Tribes in Muskogee, Oklahoma.
It was estimated that nearly a
third of museums in possession
of Indigenous artifacts would
struggle to authenticate them.
IACA has also been criticized
for its reliance on tribal
enrollment as the ultimate
arbiter of who is and who is not
legally defined as an Indigenous
American. See William J. Haipuk
Jr., "Of Kitsch and Kachinas: A
Critical Analysis of the 'Indian
Arts and Crafts Act of 1990,'"
Stanford Law Review 53, no. 4
(April 2001), 1,009–1,075, https://
doi.org/10.2307/1229497.

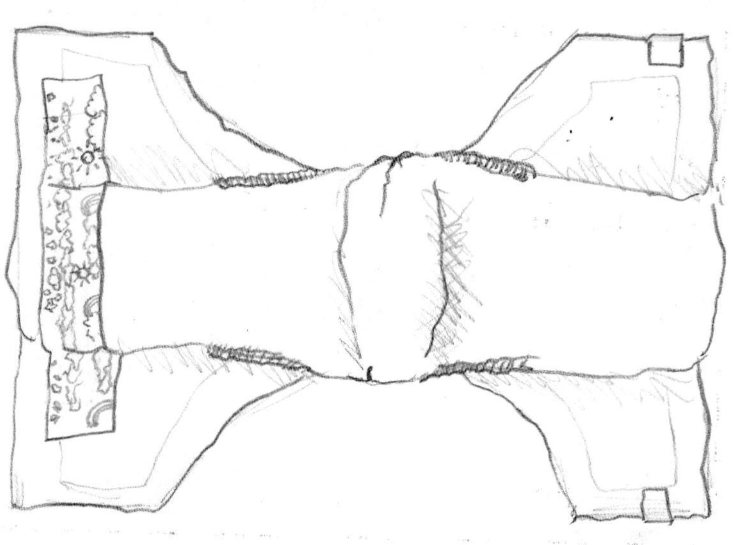

FIELD MUSEUM OF NATURAL HISTORY—ETHNOLOGY   2-2

Provenience: Toksook Bay, Nelson Is., Alaska

People or Culture: Yupik Eskimo

Object: disposable diapers

Material: –

Description: decorated waistband (2).

 Used as gift in seal party.

Dimensions: –
(in cm.)

Collection: Dr. Ann Fienup-Riordan

SWEET BITTER LOVE

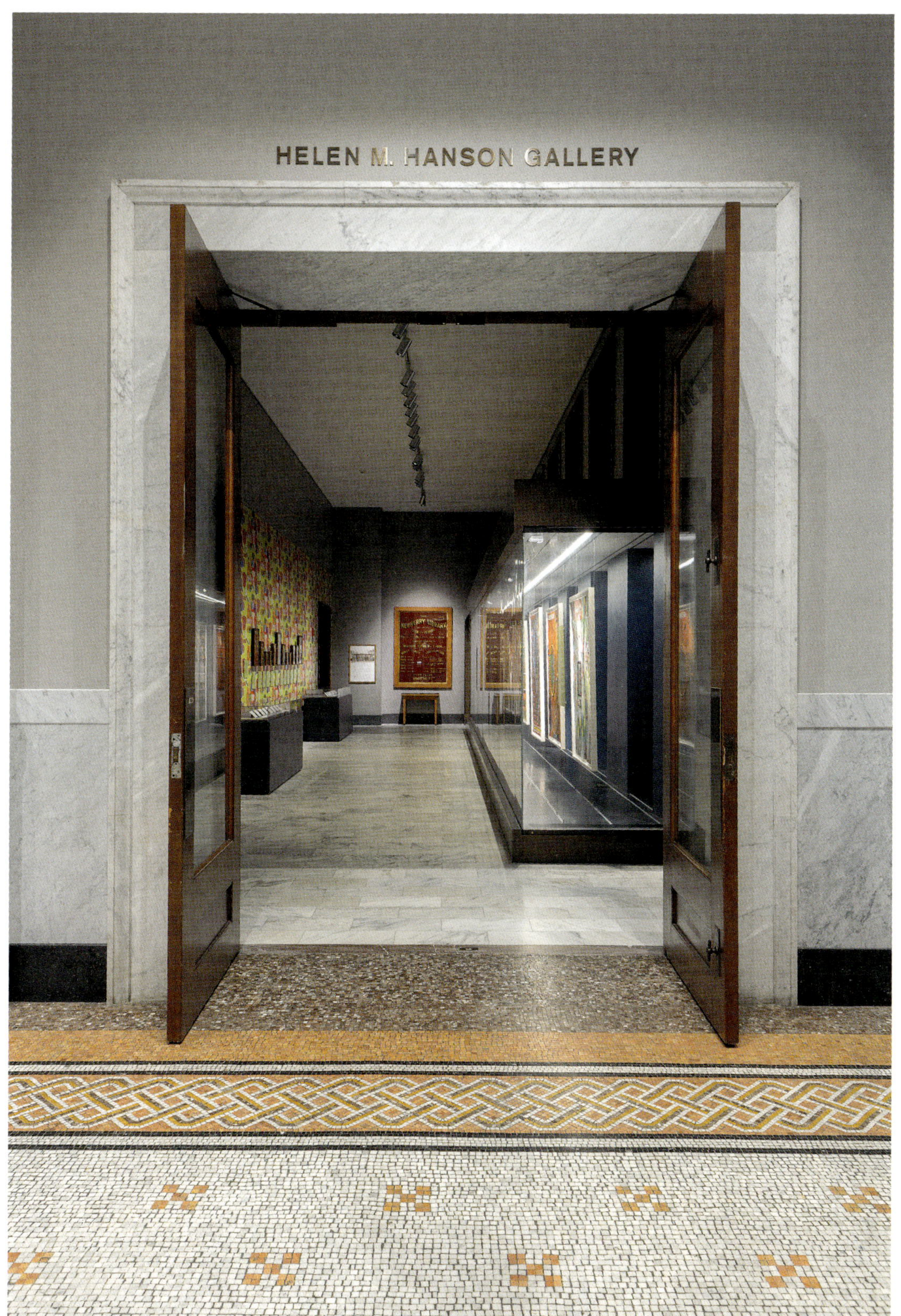
HELEN M. HANSON GALLERY

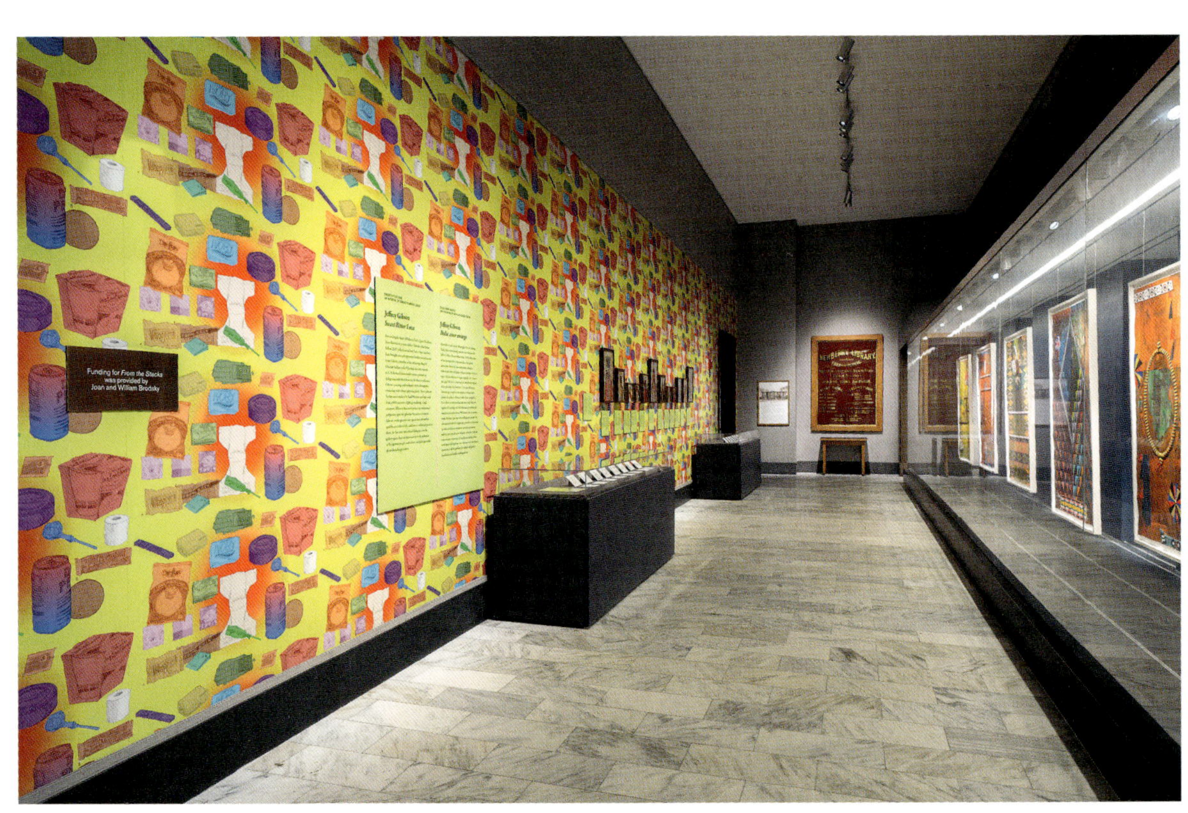

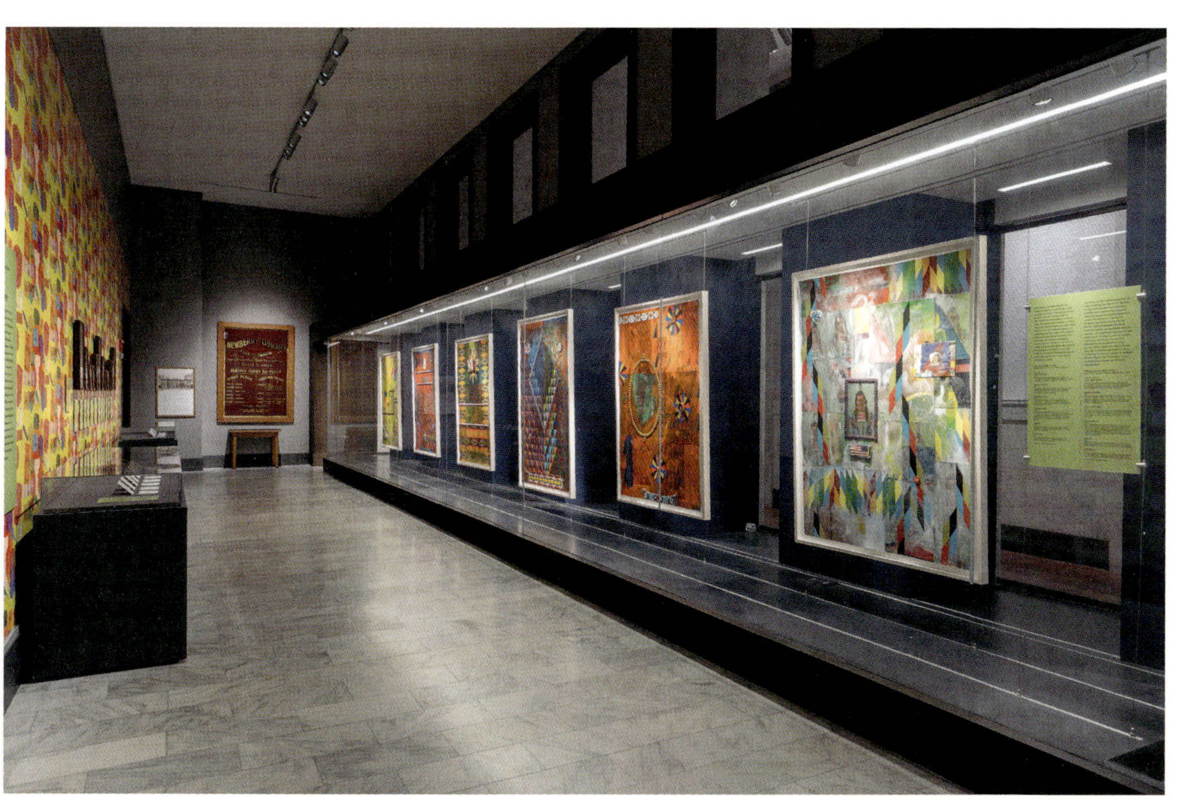

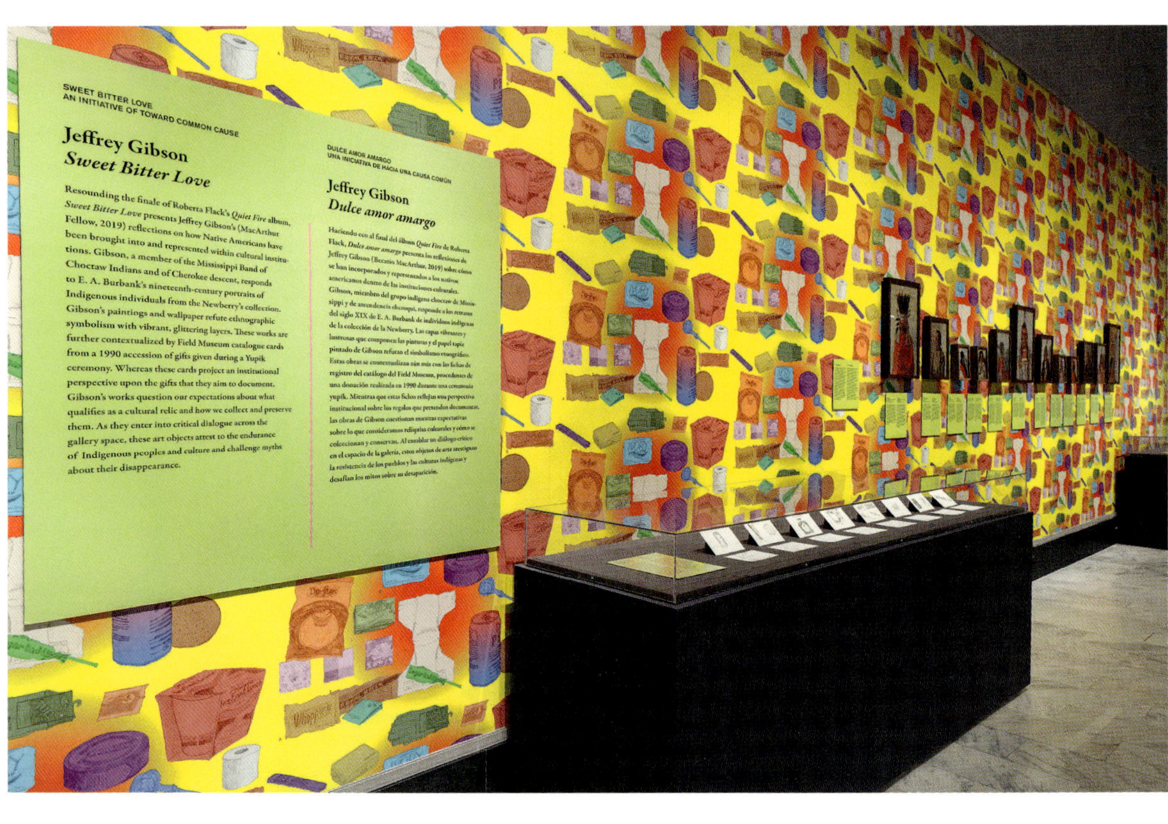

SWEET BITTER LOVE
AN INITIATIVE OF TOWARD COMMON CAUSE

Jeffrey Gibson
Sweet Bitter Love

Resounding the finale of Roberta Flack's Quiet Fire album, Sweet Bitter Love presents Jeffrey Gibson's (MacArthur Fellow, 2019) reflections on how Native Americans have been brought into and represented within cultural institutions. Gibson, a member of the Mississippi Band of Choctaw Indians and of Cherokee descent, responds to E. A. Burbank's nineteenth-century portraits of Indigenous individuals from the Newberry's collection. Gibson's paintings and wallpaper refute ethnographic symbolism with vibrant, glittering layers. These works are further contextualized by Field Museum catalogue cards from a 1990 accession of gifts given during a Yupik ceremony. Whereas these cards project an institutional perspective upon the gifts that they aim to document, Gibson's works question our expectations about what qualifies as a cultural relic and how we collect and preserve them. As they enter into critical dialogue across the gallery space, these art objects attest to the endurance of Indigenous peoples and culture and challenge myths about their disappearance.

DULCE AMOR AMARGO
UNA INICIATIVA DE HACIA UNA CAUSA COMÚN

Jeffrey Gibson
Dulce amor amargo

Haciendo eco al final del álbum Quiet Fire de Roberta Flack, Dulce amor amargo presenta las reflexiones de Jeffrey Gibson (Becario MacArthur, 2019) sobre cómo se han incorporados y representados a los nativos americanos dentro de las instituciones culturales. Gibson, miembro del grupo indígena choctaw de Mississippi y de ascendencia cheroqui, responde a los retratos del siglo XIX de E. A. Burbank de individuos indígenas de la colección de la Newberry. Las capas vibrantes y lustrosas que componen las pinturas y el papel tapiz pintado de Gibson refutan el simbolismo etnográfico. Estas obras se contextualizan aún más con las fichas de registro del catálogo del Field Museum, procedentes de una donación realizada en 1990 durante una ceremonia yupik. Mientras que estas fichas reflejan una perspectiva institucional sobre los regalos que pretenden documentar, las obras de Gibson cuestionan nuestras expectativas sobre lo que consideramos reliquias culturales y cómo se coleccionan y conservan. Al entablar un diálogo crítico en el espacio de la galería, estos objetos de arte atestiguan la resistencia de los pueblos y las culturas indígenas y desafían los mitos sobre su desaparición.

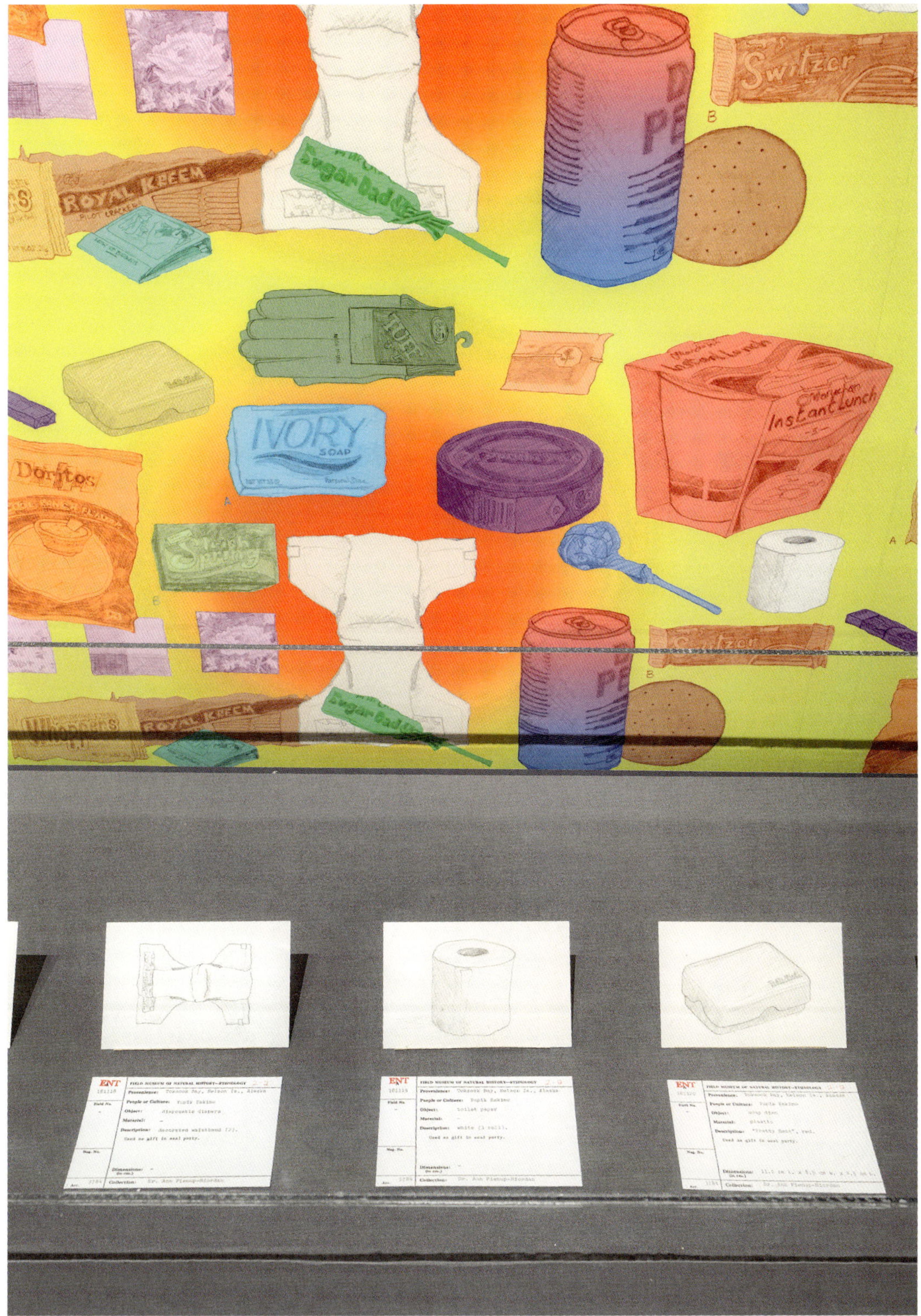

ROYAL KREEM
Switzer
DR PE
Sugar Daddy
TUFF
IVORY SOAP
Doritos
Instant Lunch
Starch
Switzer
WHOPPERS
ROYAL KREEM
Sugar Daddy
DR PE
ENT   FIELD MUSEUM OF NATURAL HISTORY—ETHNOLOGY
ENT   FIELD MUSEUM OF NATURAL HISTORY—ETHNOLOGY
ENT   FIELD MUSEUM OF NATURAL HISTORY—ETHNOLOGY

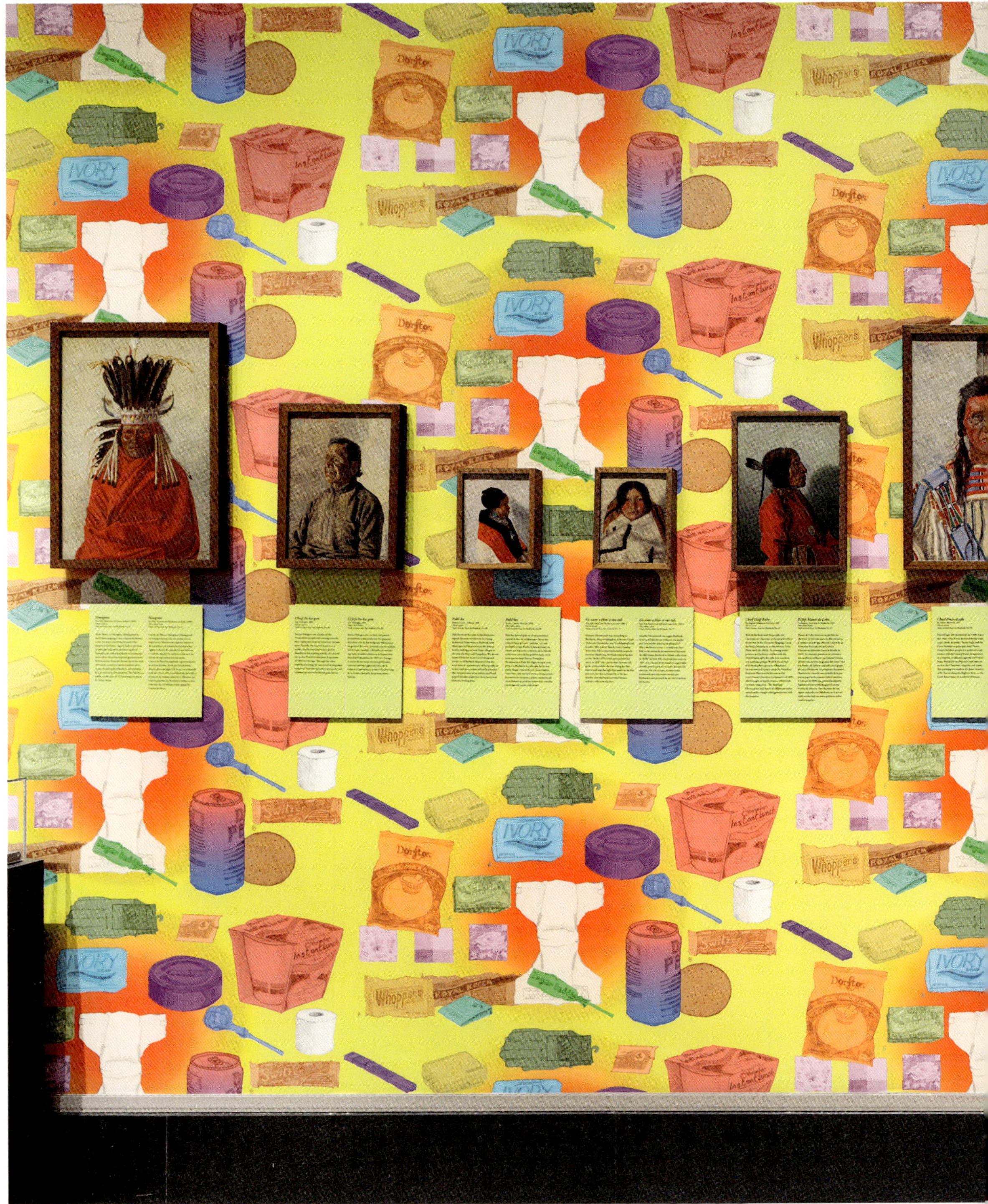

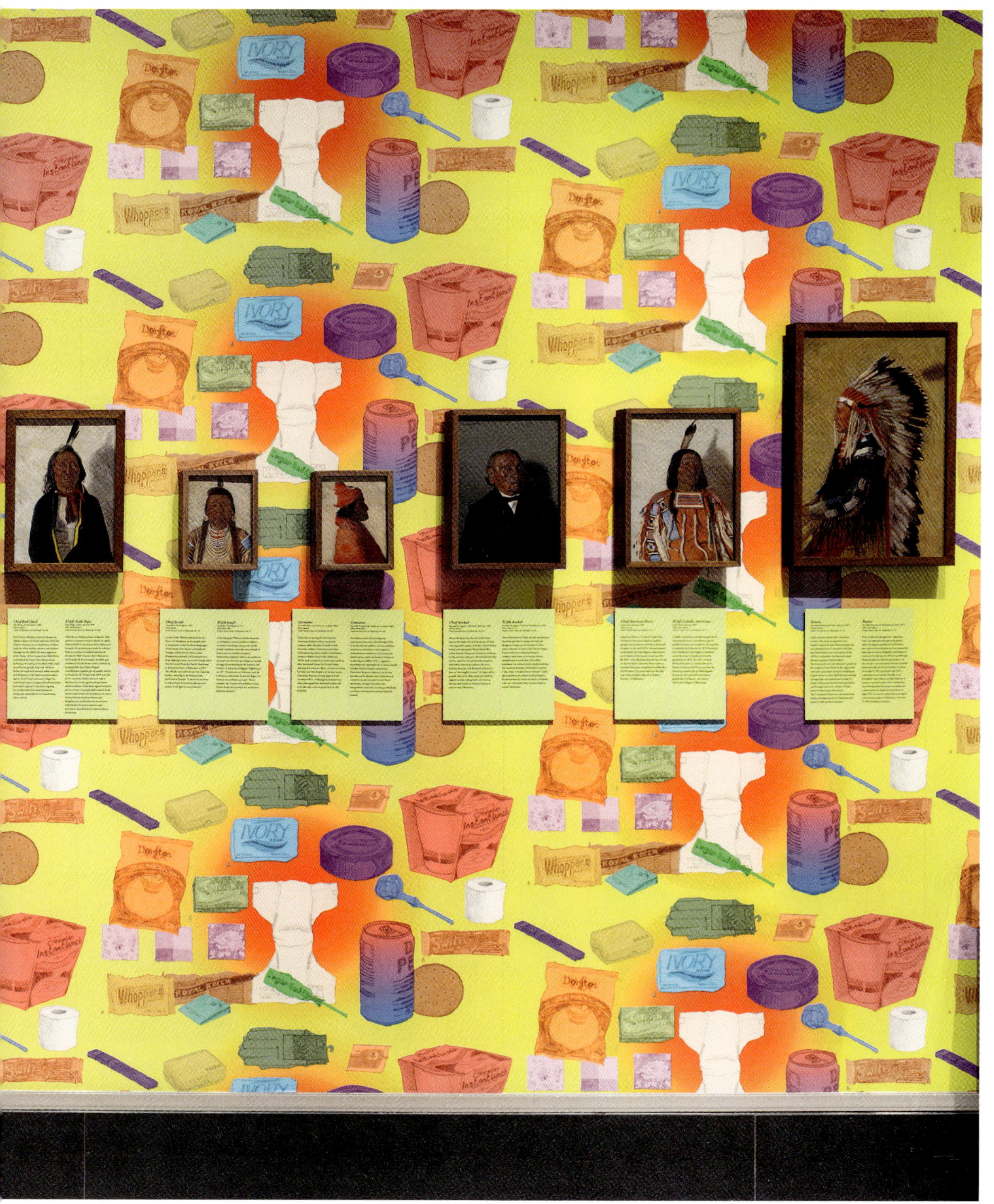

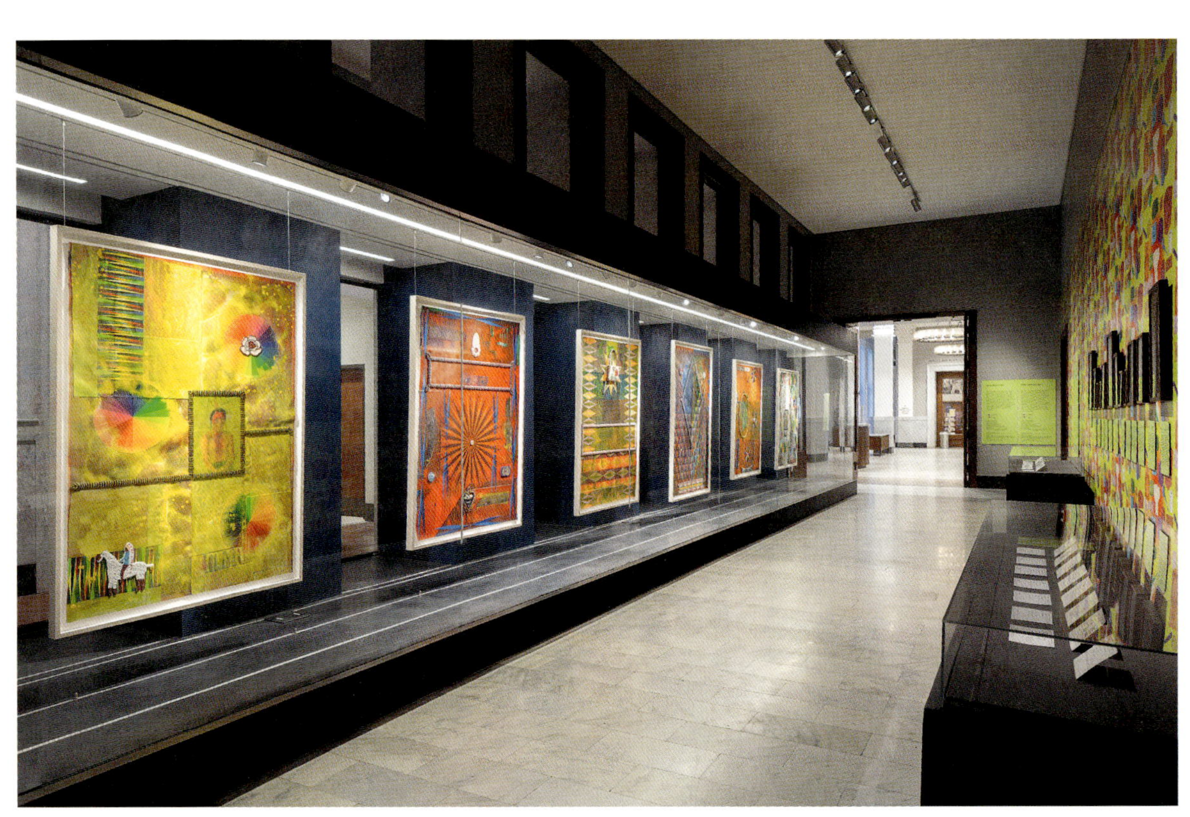

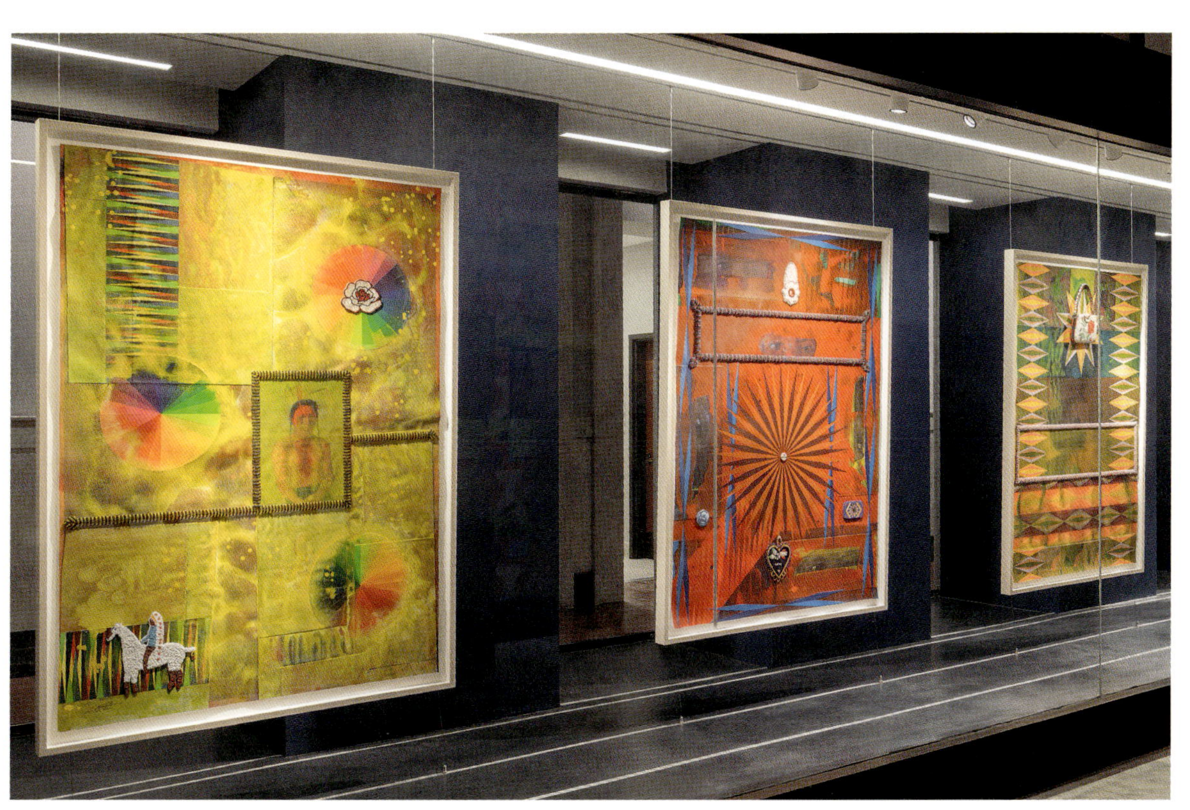

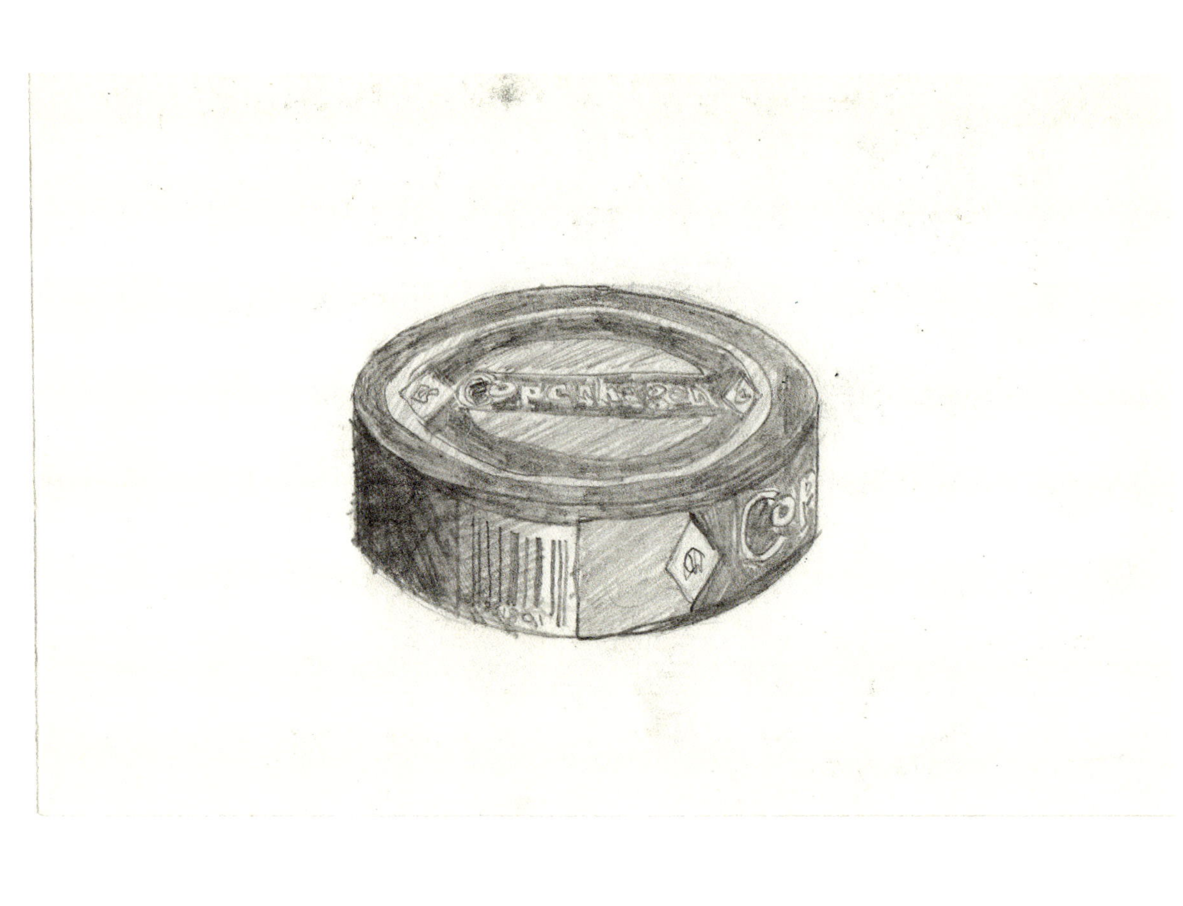
Copenhagen
Cop

181116

Field No.

–

Neg. No.

Acc. 3784

FIELD MUSEUM OF NATURAL HISTORY—ETHNOLOGY   2-22

Provenience: Toksook Bay, Nelson Is., Alaska

People or Culture: Yupik Eskimo

Object: snuff

Material: –

Description: "Copenhagen" (1 tin - 1.2 oz.)

Used as gift in seal party.

Dimensions: –
(in cm.)

Collection: Dr. Ann Fienup-Riordan

41

PLATES: BURBANK

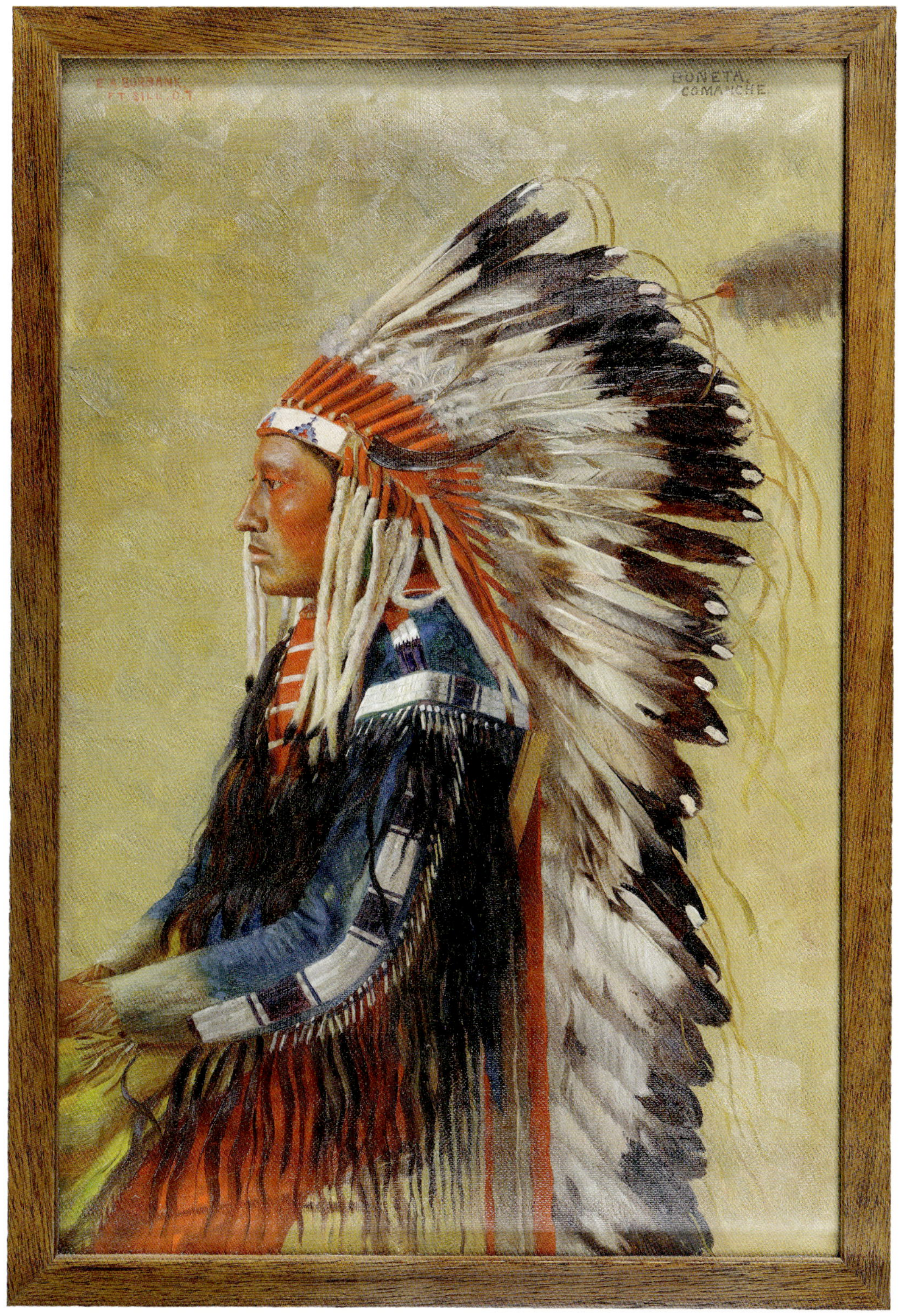

E. A. BURBANK
FT. SILL O.T.
BONETA,
COMANCHE

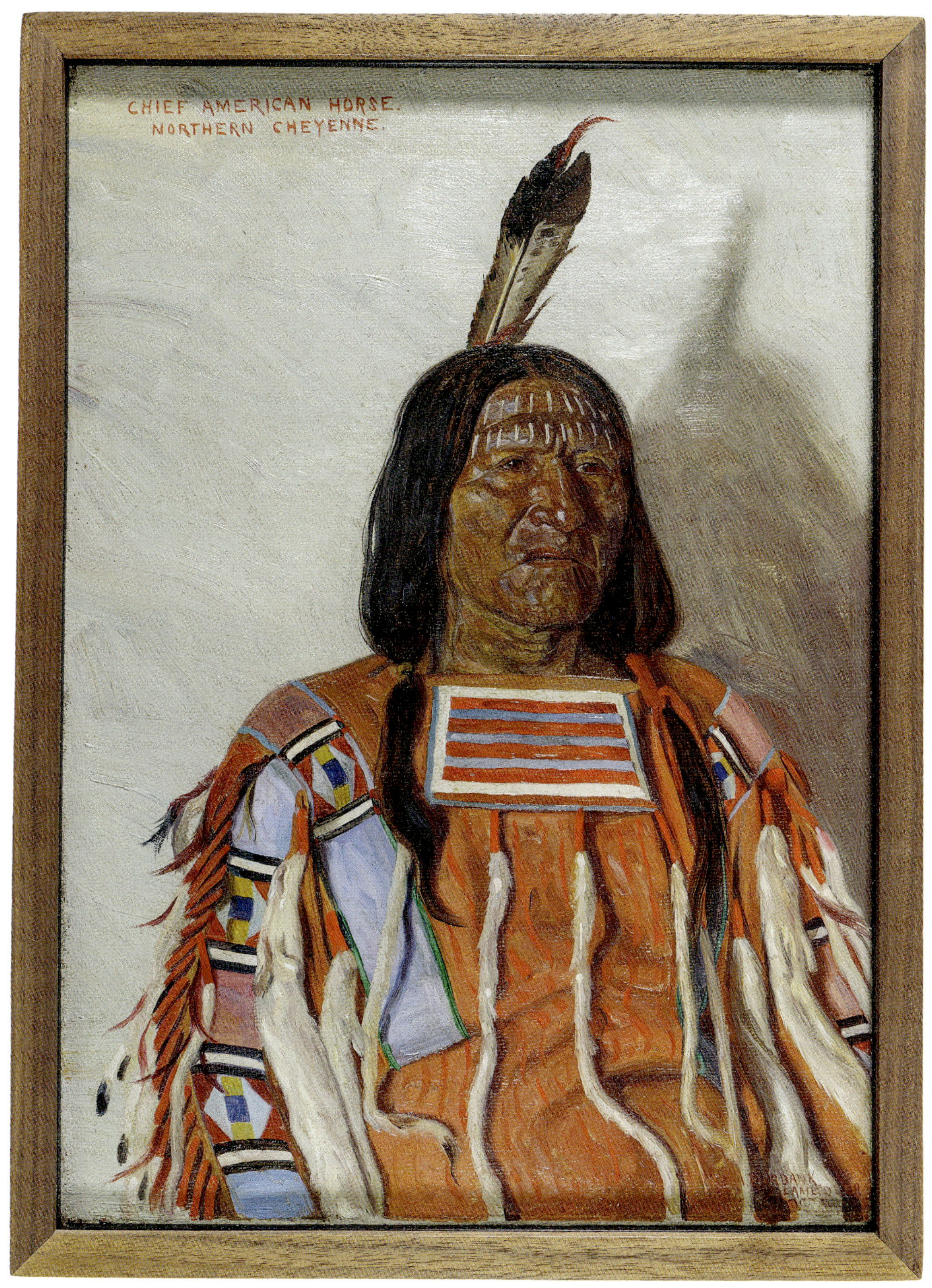
CHIEF AMERICAN HORSE.
NORTHERN CHEYENNE.

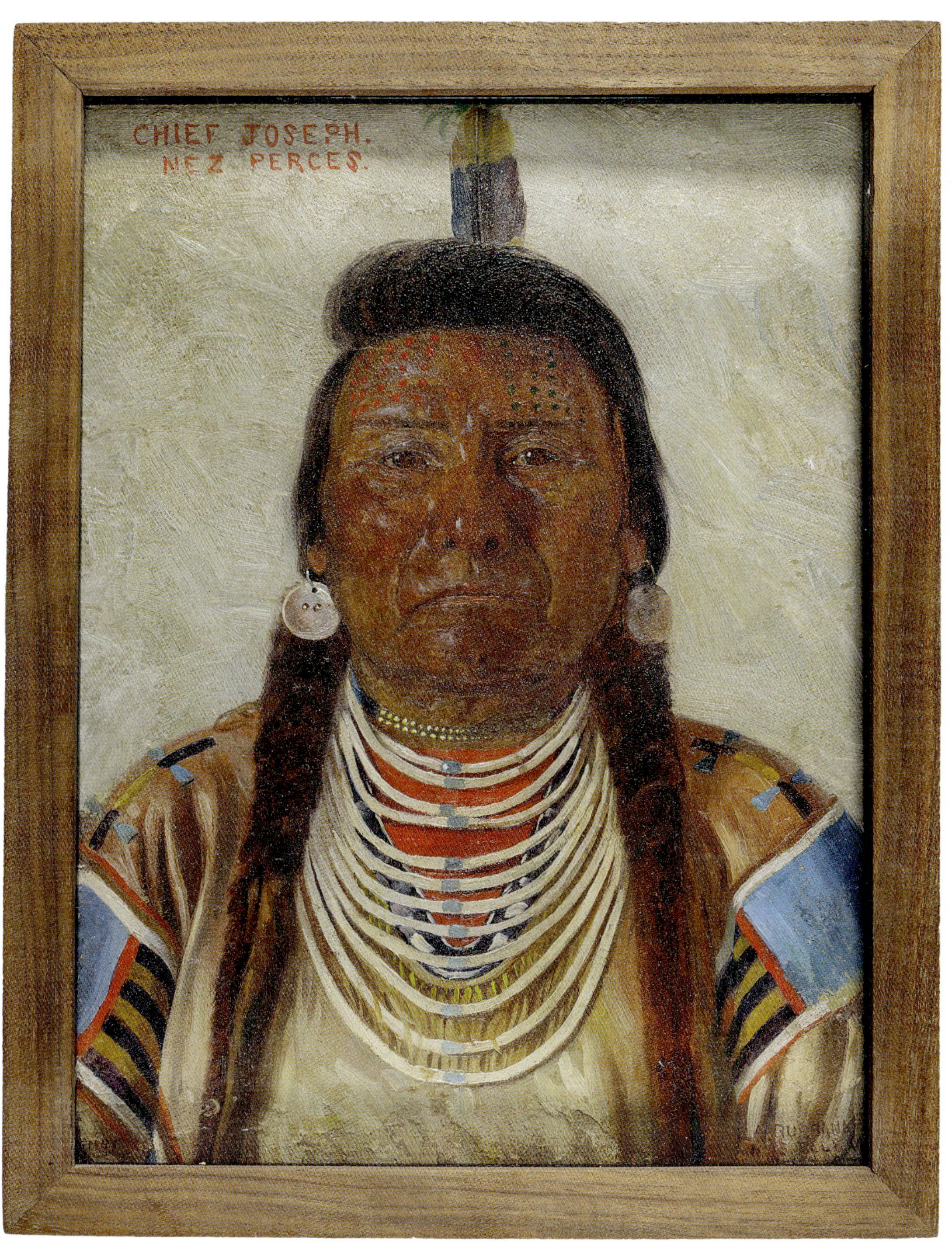
CHIEF JOSEPH.
NEZ PERCES.

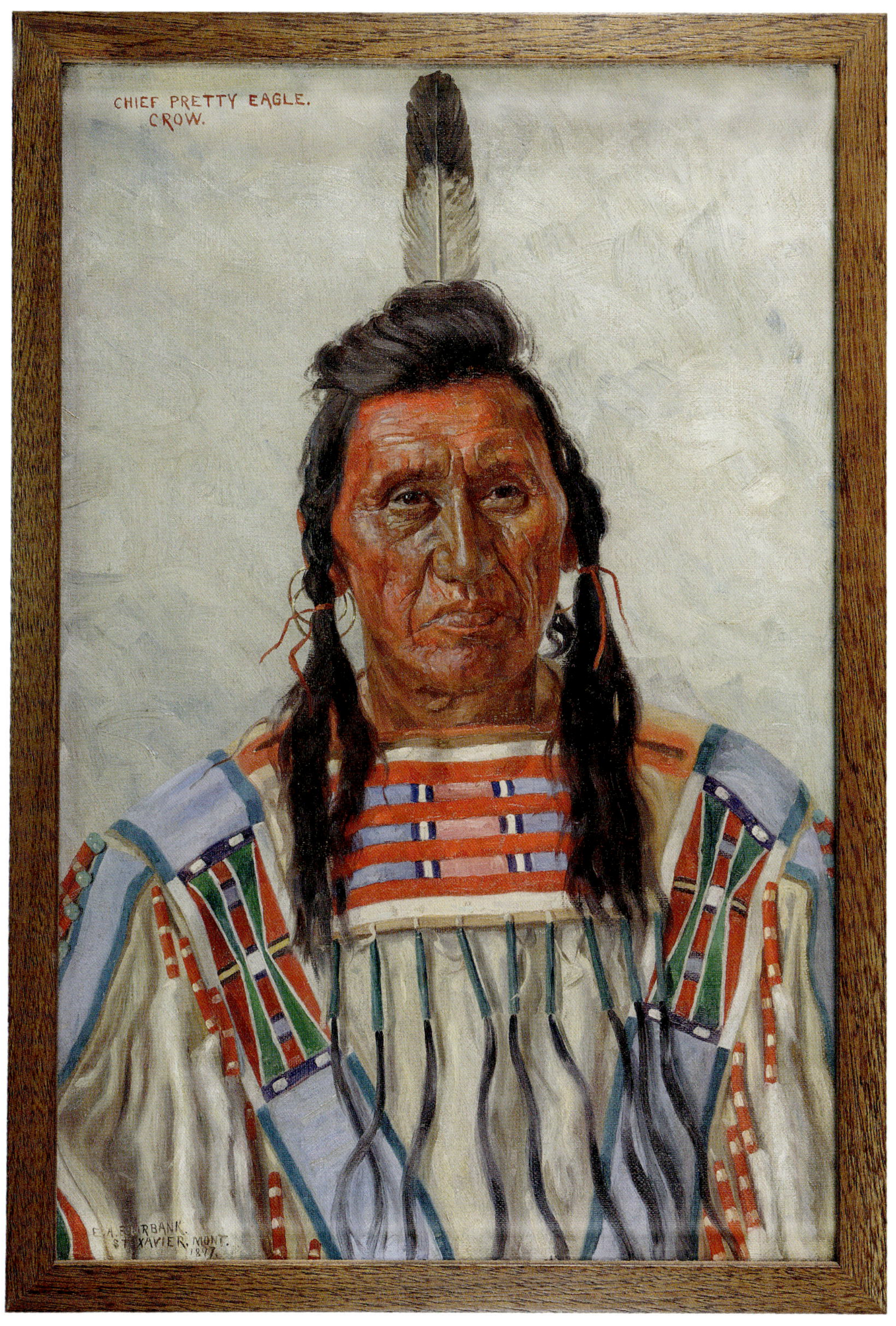
CHIEF PRETTY EAGLE.
CROW.
E.A. FAIRBANK.
ST XAVIER, MONT.
1897.

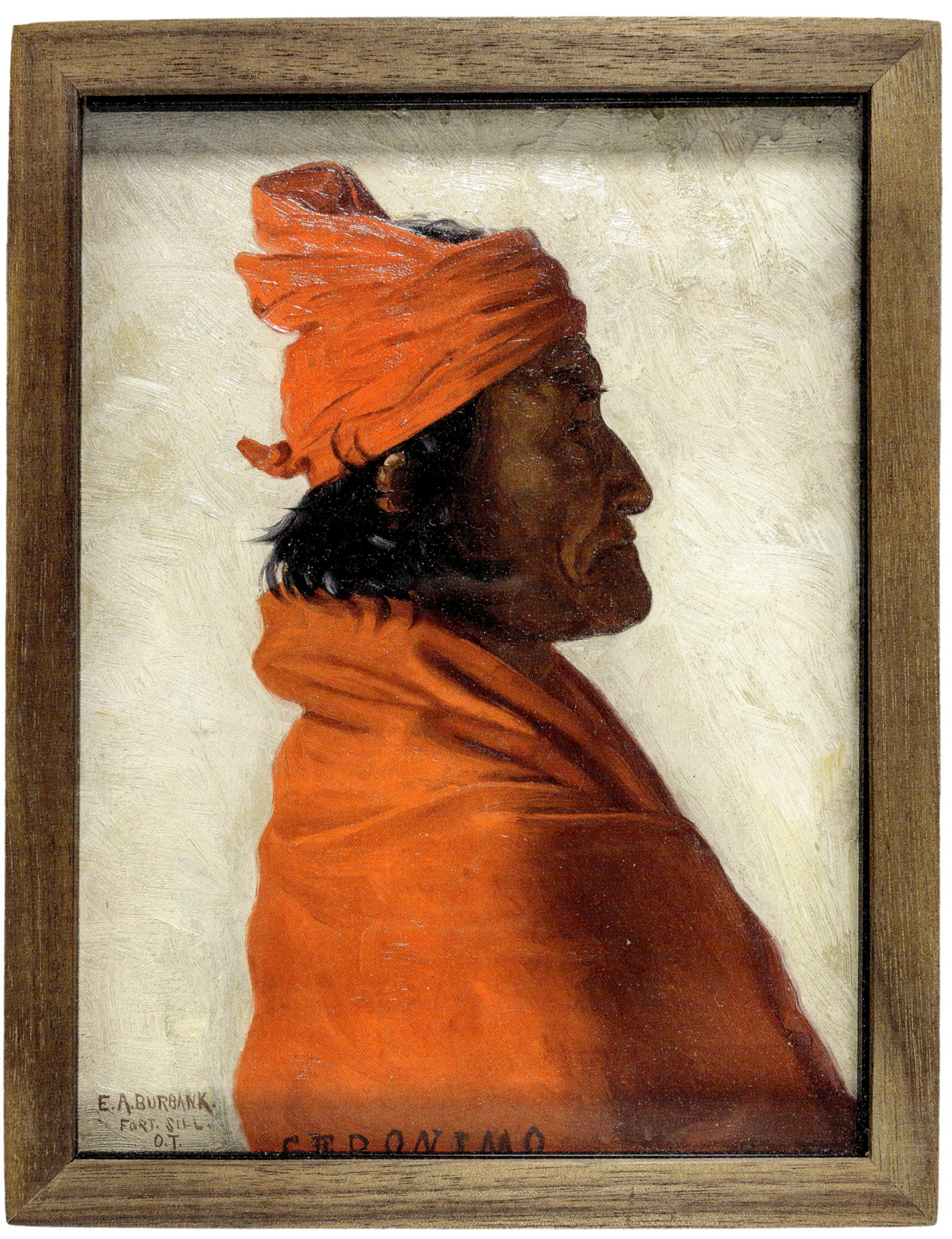

E.A.BURBANK
FORT. SILL.
O.T.
GERONIMO

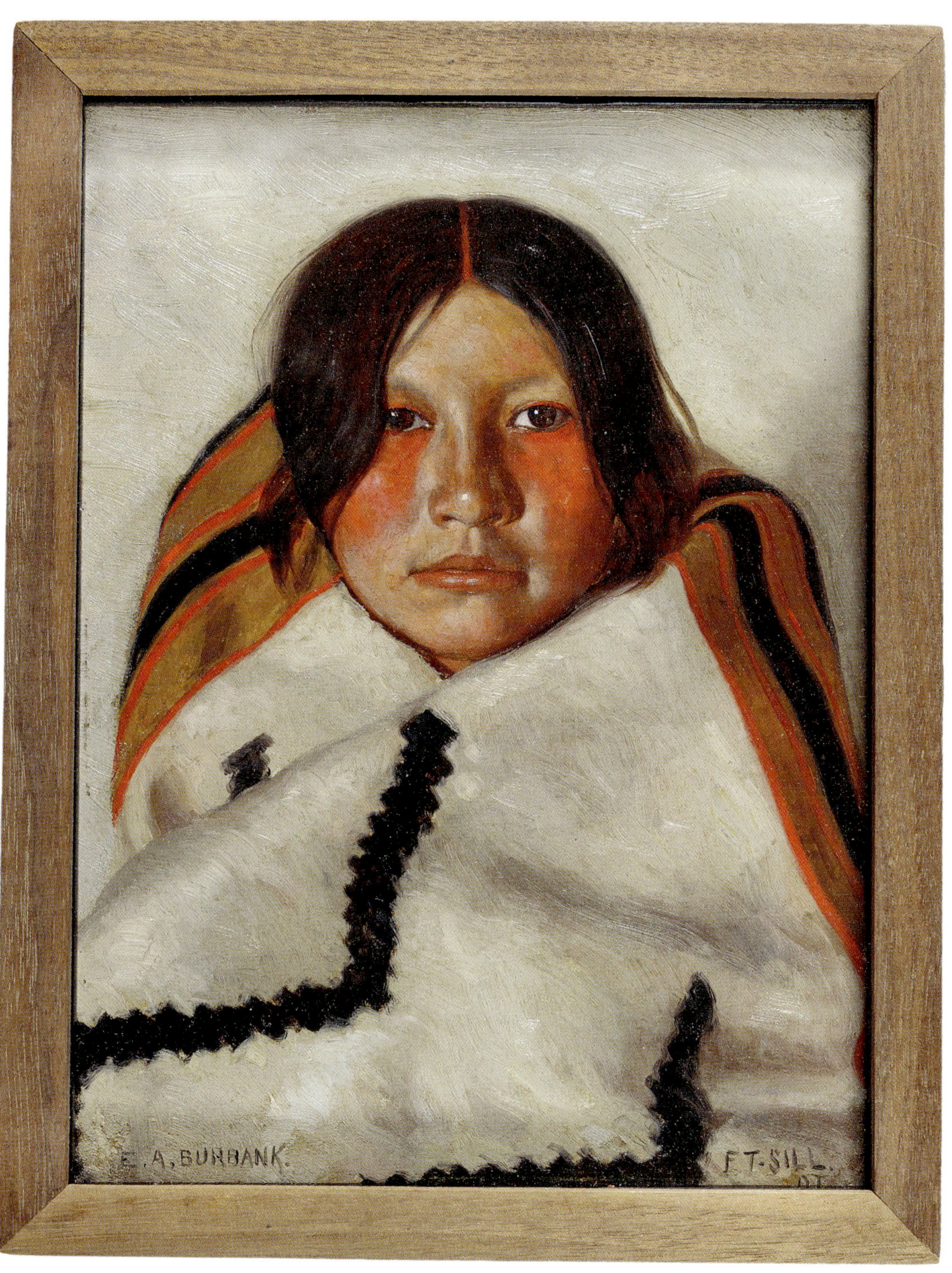

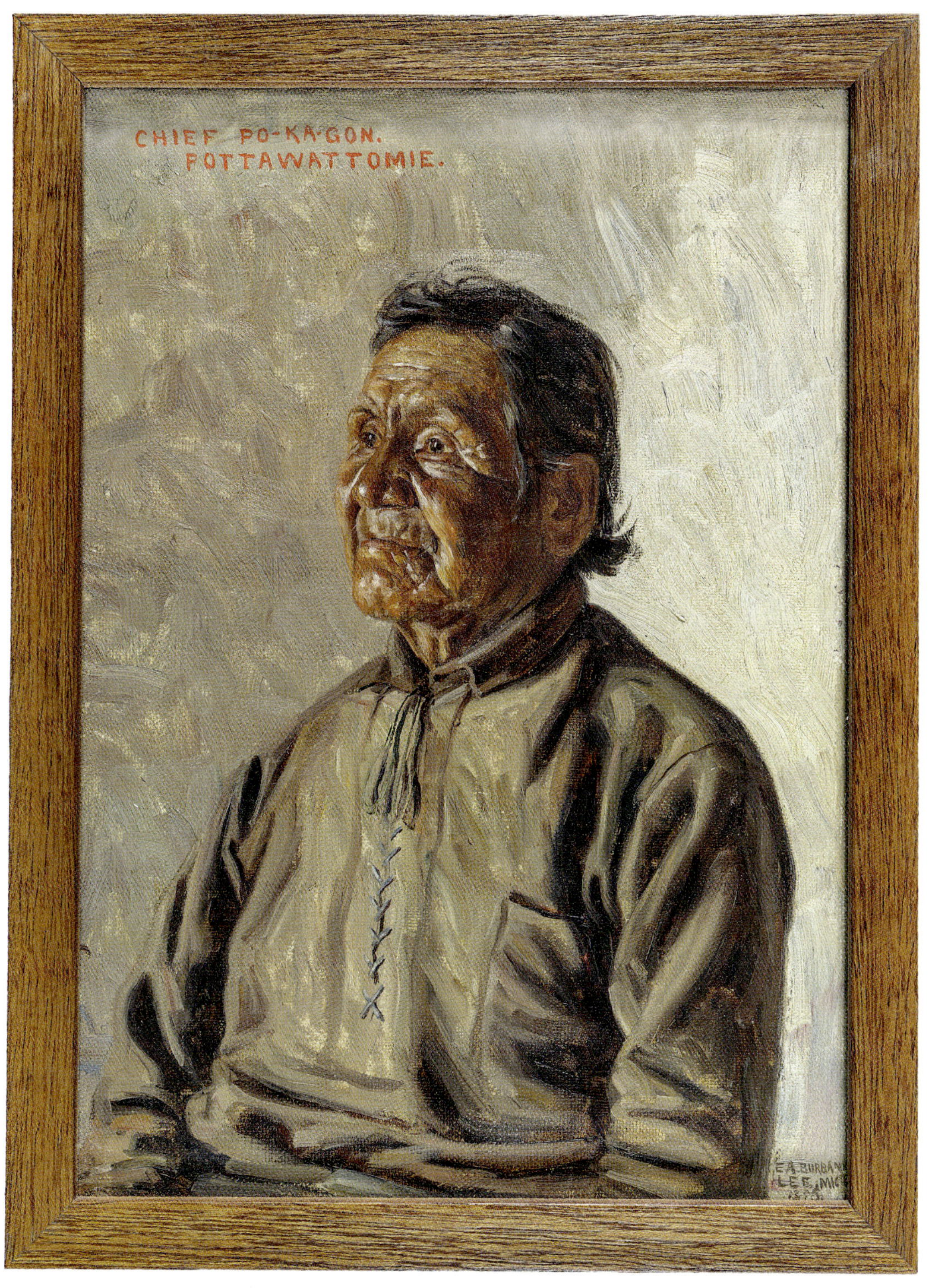
CHIEF PO-KA-GON.
POTTAWATTOMIE.

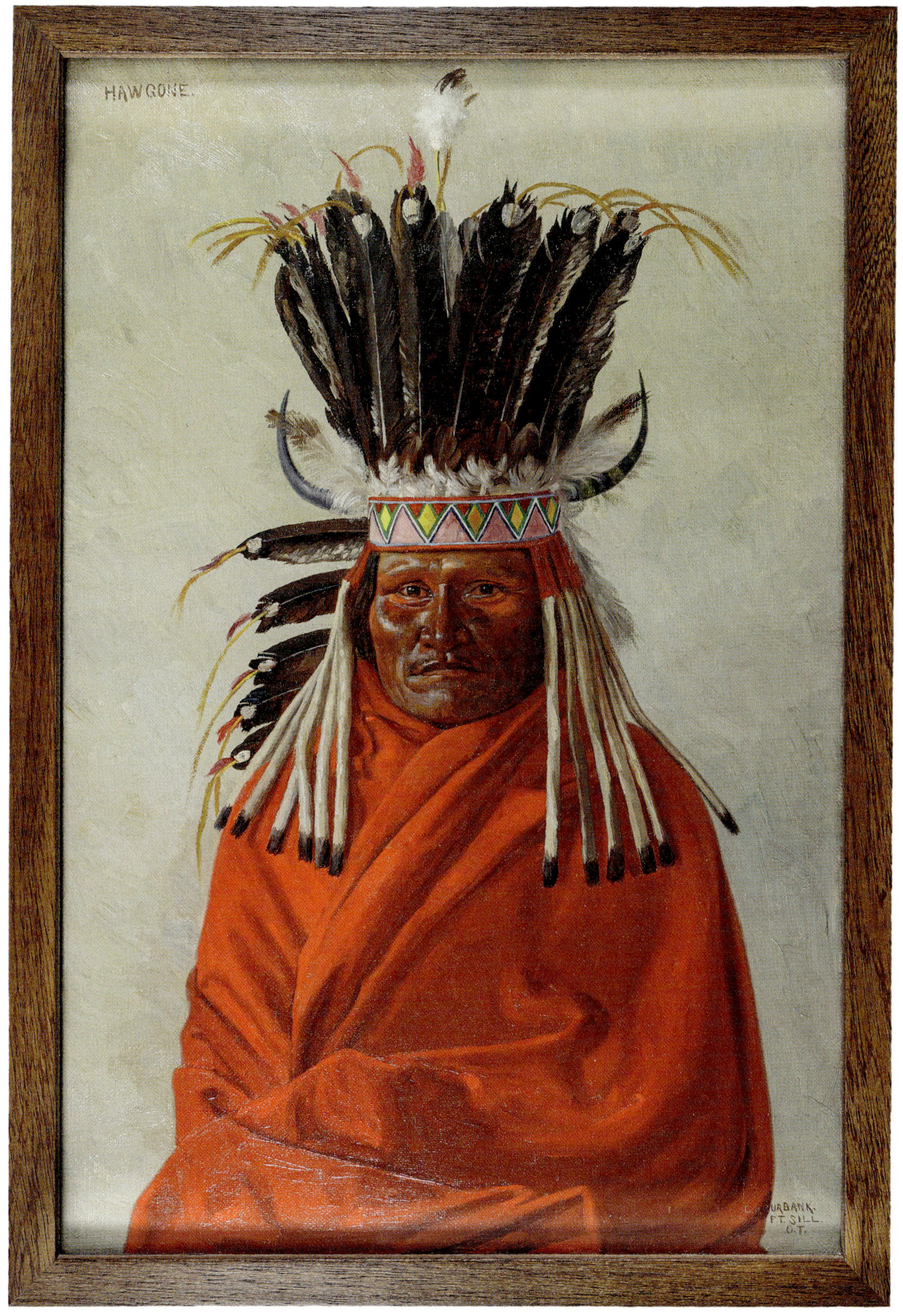

HAWGONE.

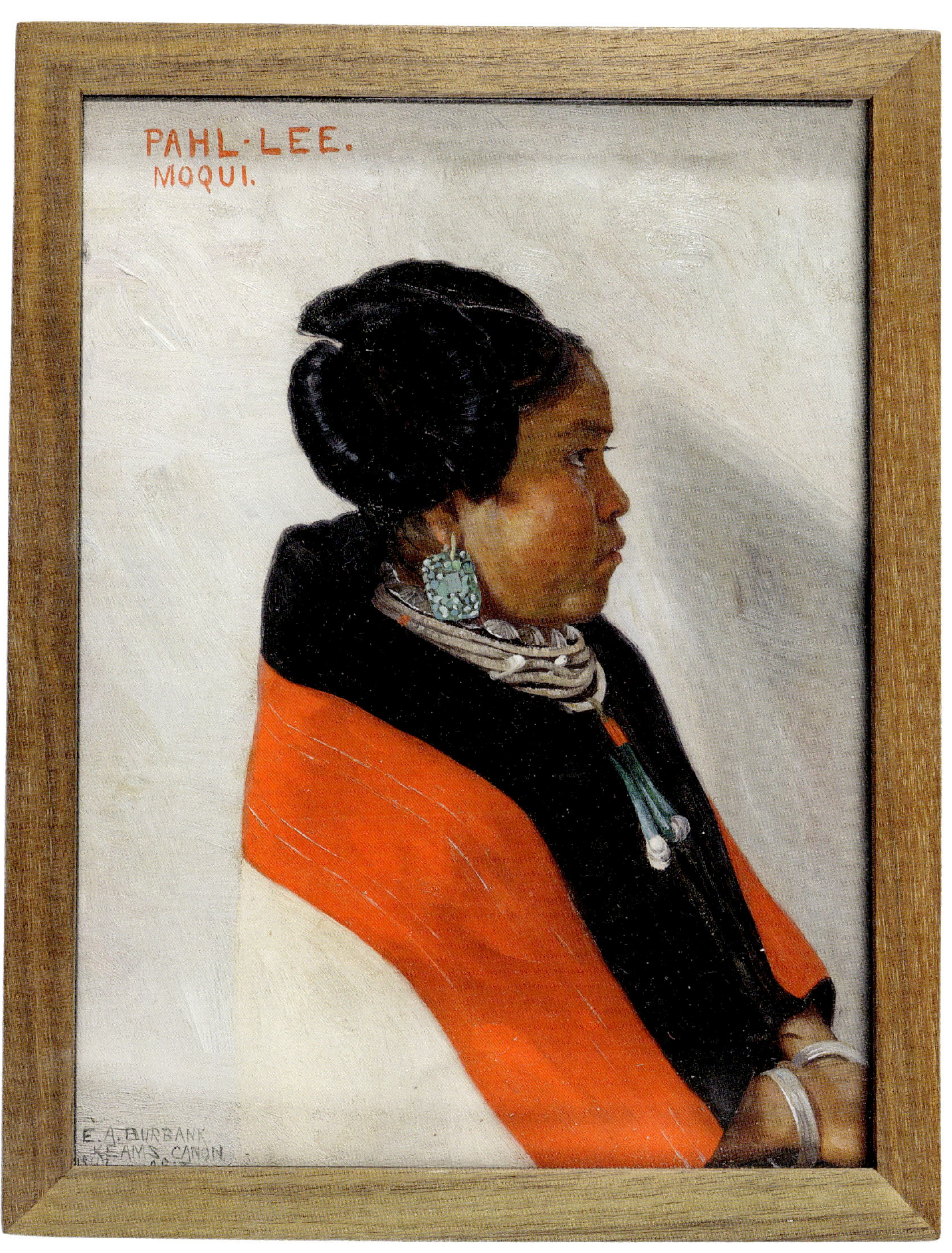

PAHL·LEE·
MOQUI.
E. A. BURBANK
KEAMS CANON

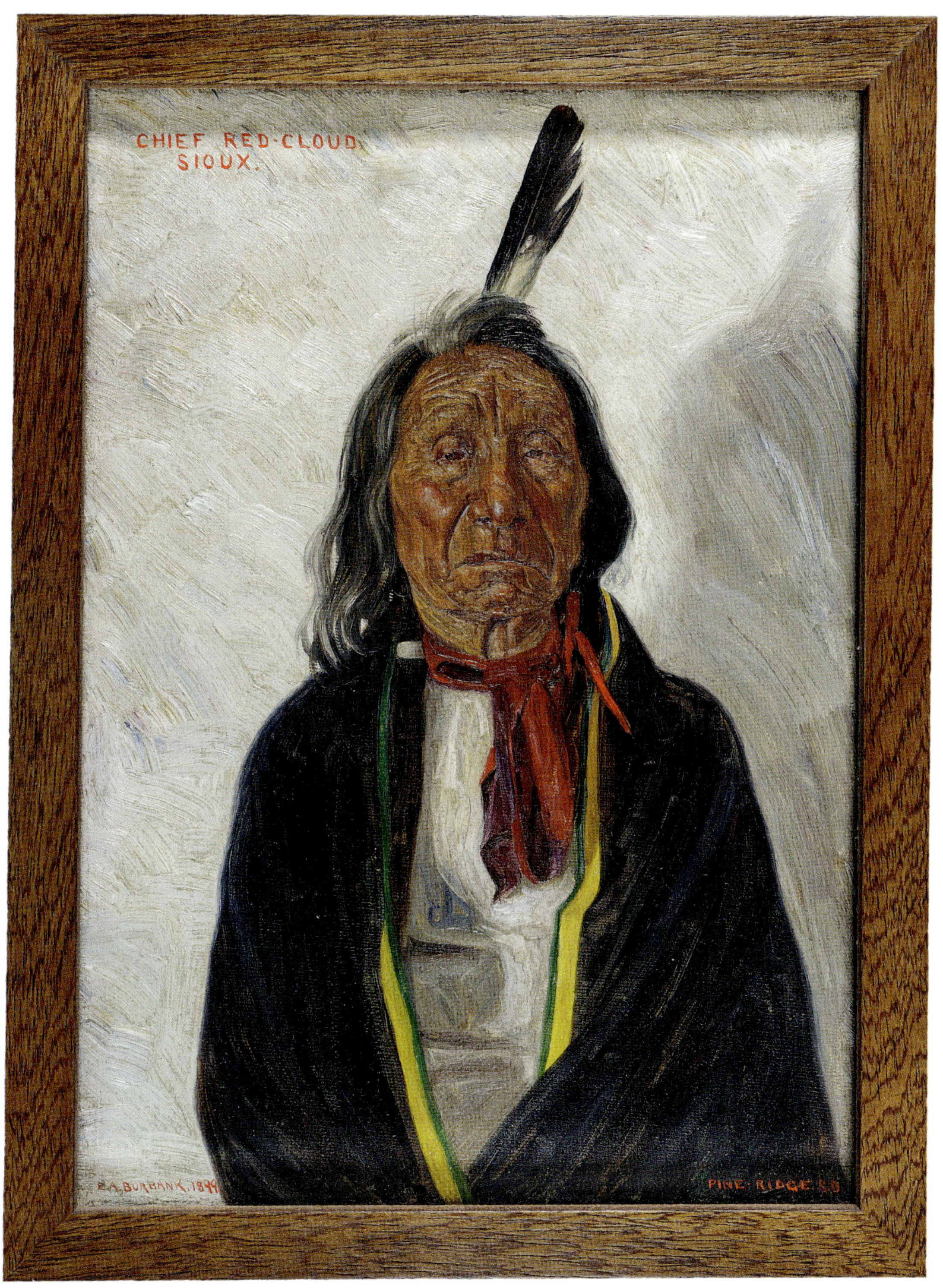
CHIEF RED-CLOUD,
SIOUX.
E.A.BURBANK 1899
PINE-RIDGE S.D.

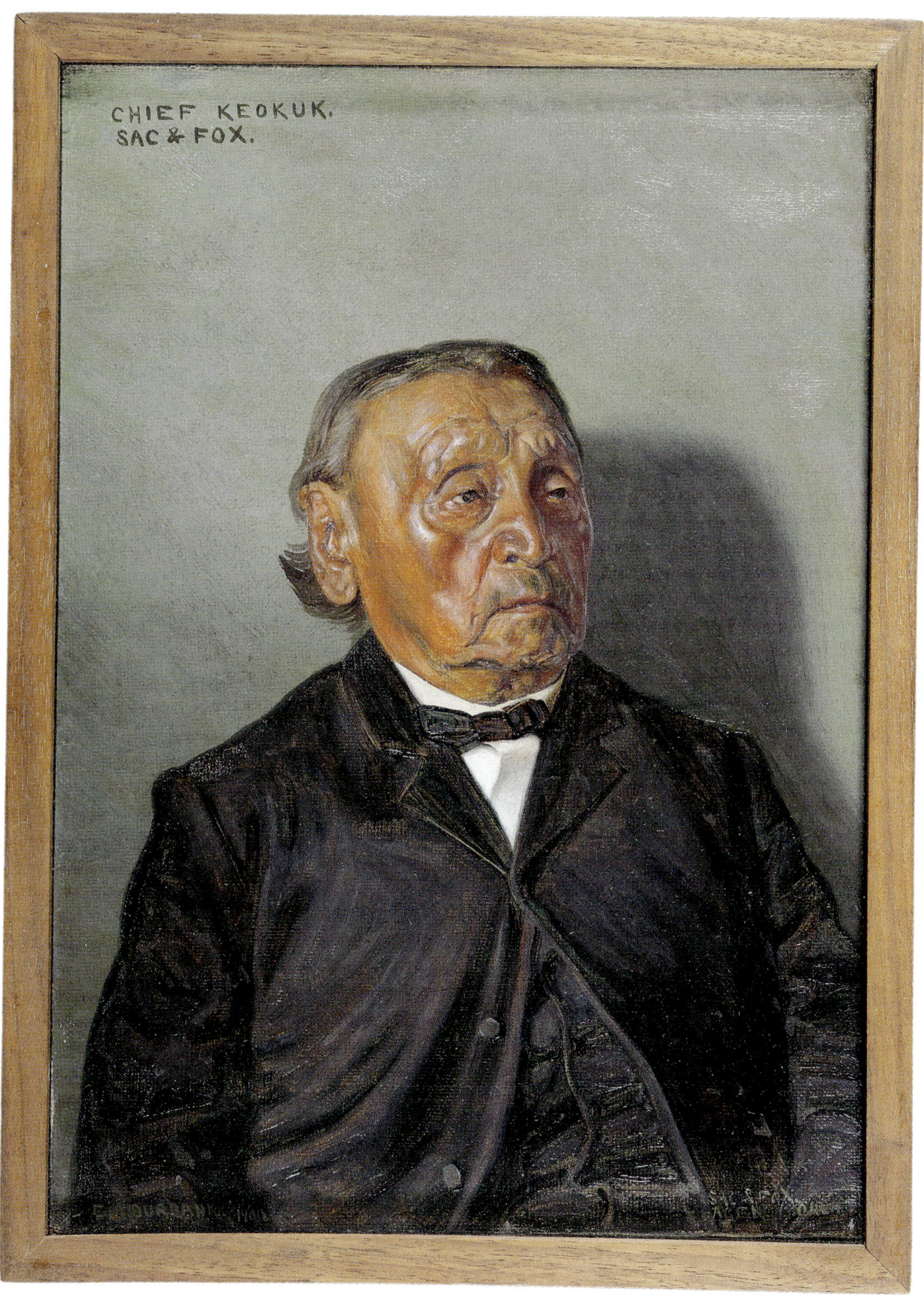

CHIEF KEOKUK.
SAC & FOX.

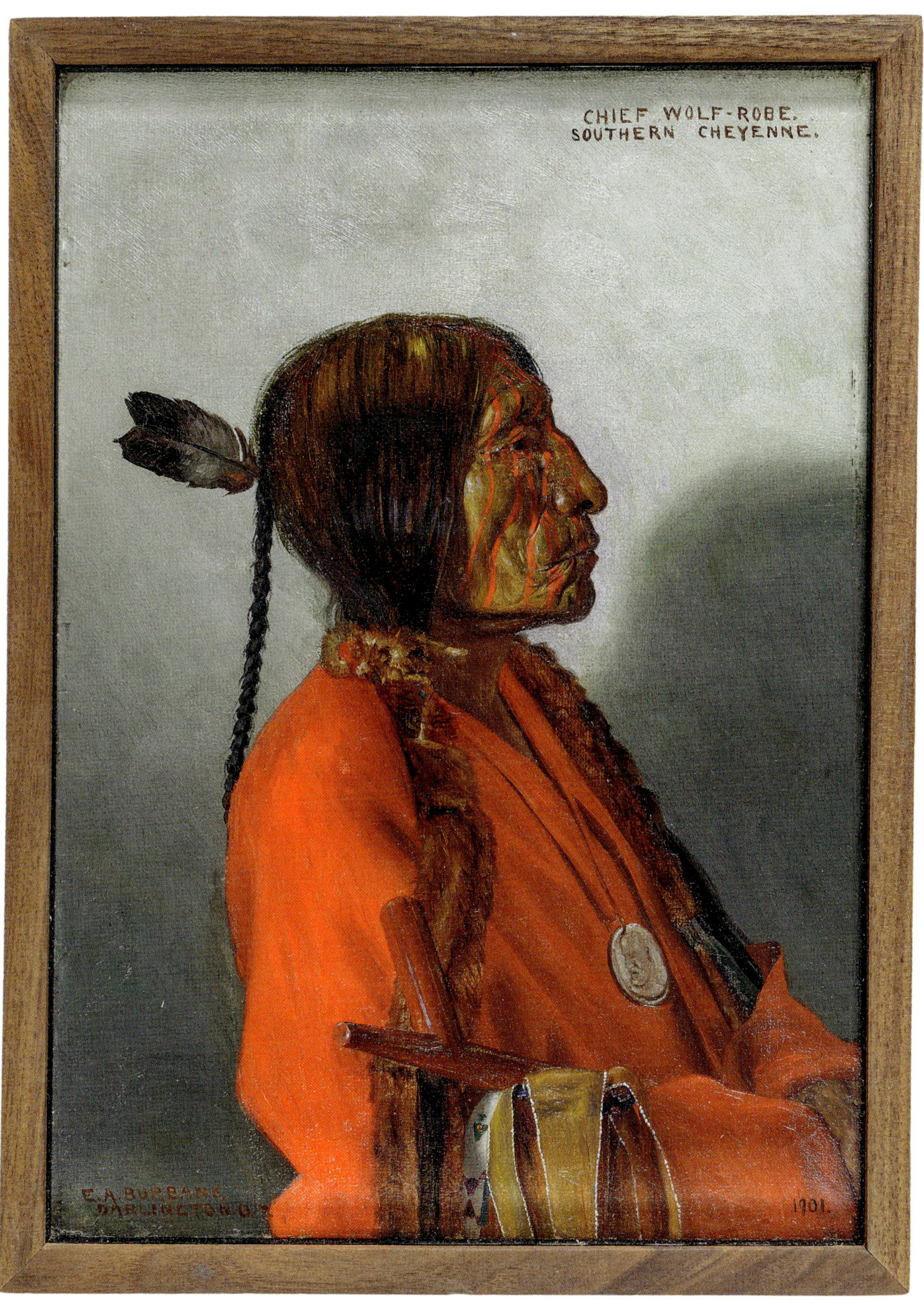

CHIEF WOLF-ROBE.
SOUTHERN CHEYENNE.
E.A.BURBANK
DARLINGTON O.T.
1901.

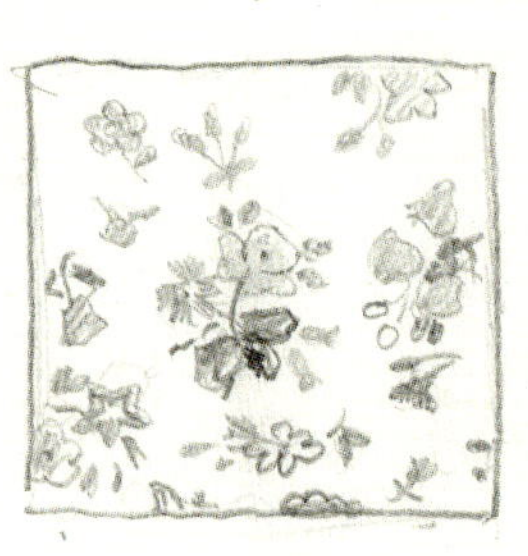 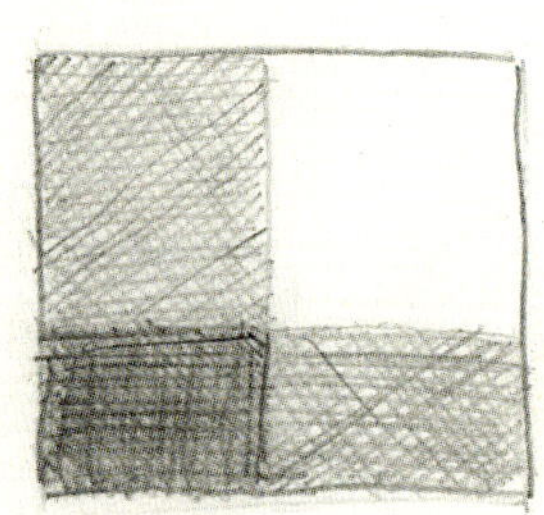 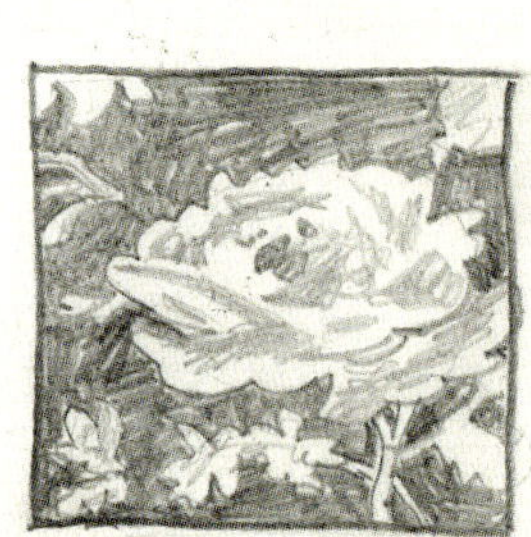

samples of all three

FIELD MUSEUM OF NATURAL HISTORY—ETHNOLOGY 2-2?

Provenience: Toksook Bay, Nelson Is., Alaska

People or Culture: Yupik Eskimo

Object: cloth

Material: cotton

Description: rectangular lengths –
multi-colored floral (2),
blue & white checked (1),
gold-flowered on blue (1).

Used as gift in seal party.

Dimensions: −
(in cm.)

Collection: Dr. Ann Fienup-Riordan

THE BLISS POINT: JEFFREY GIBSON PROCESSING AUTHENTIC AMERICAN PASTS

CHRISTIAN AYNE CROUCH

The John D. and Catherine T. MacArthur Foundation, which awarded Jeffrey Gibson a MacArthur Fellowship in 2019, has been head-quartered in Chicago's landmarked Marquette Building since the 1970s. With its Beaux-Arts ornamentation by Hermon A. MacNeil, the structure is an 1893 festival of "more is more" decorative application. A celebration of Euro-American intrusion into the homelands of the Anishinaabeg and several other Indigenous nations, rendered as four bronze friezes, presides over the Marquette Building's four doors.[1] Fleur-de-lis, acanthus leaf, rosettes, owl eyes, and Greek key patterns bedeck the bronze front door frames; plaques in the shapes of hatchets and calumets join lions in profile on the handles. The friezes capture the moment of Father Jacques Marquette's arrival along the Chicago River. Perhaps concerned that future histories might fail to give the Jesuit his due, MacNeil surmounted the door façade with "MARQUETTE" and provided extracts of Marquette's diary in capital letters beneath each frieze. Even if most of the figures appear to represent Indigenous people, MacNeil spells out who should be the focus. One enters the building beneath the images of Indigenous men bearing heavy por-tage loads or European coffins or shooting arrows at the invaders (fig. 1). But though the building bombards viewers with elaborate de-signs that revel in the "civilizing" process, nowadays one's entrance comes through revolving glass doors that bear a modern "no guns" decal on the glass, a dissonant detail accentuated by the snapshot of violence just above. Gibson originally intended to produce a video project from footage taken at the building, in dialogue with *Sweet Bitter Love*, the artist's exhibition at Chicago's Newberry Library orga-nized as part of the MacArthur Foundation's *Toward Common Cause: Art, Social Change, and the MacArthur Fellows Program at 40* initiative, and to continue thinking across the spectral spaces of the city's cul-tural institutions, but the global pandemic hindered this aim.

Nonetheless, we gain insight into Gibson's perspectives both through his initial video footage and the ways in which he framed his engagement with a collection at Chicago's Field Museum of Natural History used to produce materials in *Sweet Bitter Love* and exhib-ited later in *Beyond the Horizon*, a second exhibition at Kavi Gupta, Chicago, in 2021. Field Museum Accession 3784 (fig. 2) includes bags

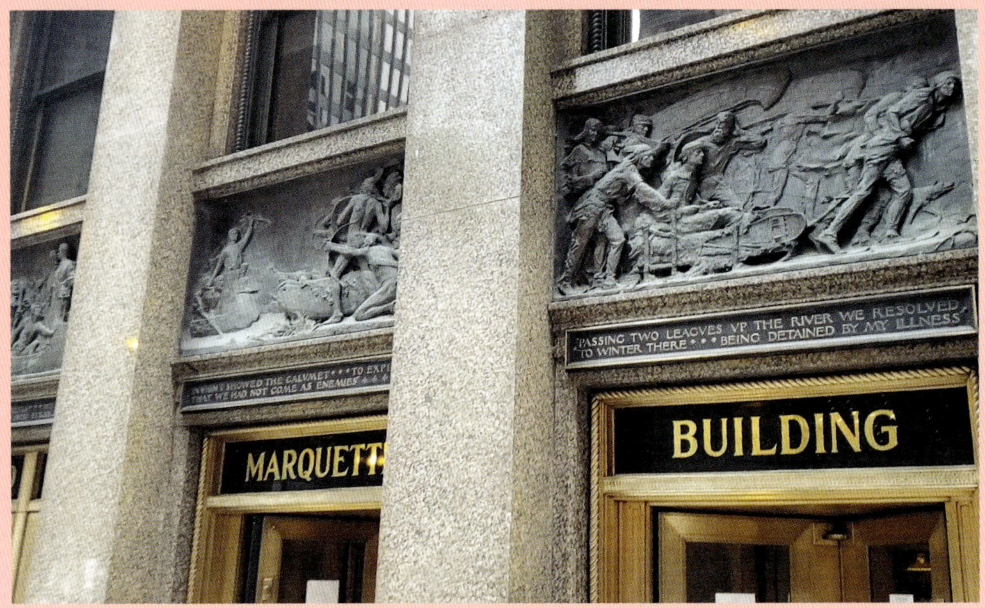

1: Exterior bronze frieze of the Marquette Building, Chicago. Designed and executed by Mr. Herman A. MacNeil, 1895. This photograph is a still from Jeffrey Gibson's scouting videos of the Marquette Building, 2020. Courtesy of Jeffrey Gibson.

of Doritos, Royal Kreem pilot crackers and Diet Pepsi, Switzer Cherry Stix and lollipops, Ivory soap and tobacco. We can't eat the food or pop the soda-can top; we can't lather the soap or spit the chew. They are preserved for posterity, many in clear plastic bags hand labeled "Do not open Inner Bag/Consult Collections Manager." Their journey to Chicago began on Nelson Island, Alaska, as gifts given at Toksook Bay by a Yup'ik mother, grandmother, and elder sister "to celebrate a five-year-old boy's first little bird (*tengmiaqsaraq*)" catch and kill.[2] Reflecting on the museum's Accession 3784, Jeffrey Gibson notes that "at the time they were being given, they were a gift of what we need," though, he observes, "we don't need candy, so there's something about a gift as a want or pleasure."[3] The accession catalogue cards and drawings that accompanied these candies when they entered the Field Museum in 1990 do not radiate that pleasure, or desire; nor do they manifest the joyfulness of giving away quotidian objects and the individual delight and interpretation of that which has been given. When the museum's clinical drawings of the candy—and of other items from that tengmiaqsaraq such as Doritos and fabric patches—begin a new chapter as a vinyl wallpaper appearing in Gibson's exhibition *Sweet Bitter Love* at the Newberry Library, and then subsequently at Gibson's *Beyond the Horizon* at Kavi Gupta (also in Chicago), this enthusiasm and unique relationship blossoms with full radiance.

Few people go to a museum to interact with institutional accession catalogue cards, though the cards form a backbone of a museum's collecting process. They do not win a place of prominence in the luxurious display halls designed to impress visitors from around the world, but instead languish in purgatorial storage as functional records of expansion. For Jeffrey Gibson, the cards from the 1990 tengmiaqsaraq and the materials they represent offer layered entrance points to invite viewers to reflect on the materials themselves and on their community context. Instead of seeing these materials as merely past—or passed—he sees them as harbingers of an evolving futurity. If taken merely on their own, the 1990–91 catalogue cards from the Field Museum impress a recording practice seated at the intersection of nineteenth-century scientific antiquarianism and the laboratory notebooks of modern science. These carefully crafted index cards

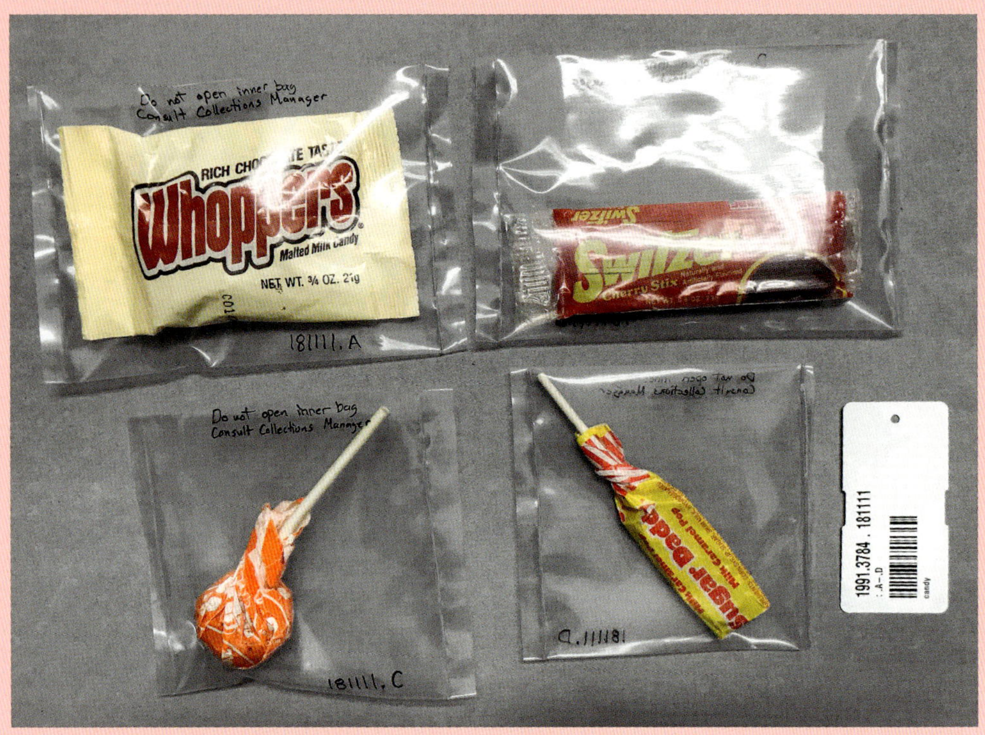

2: Field Museum Accession 3784, Nelson Island Seal Party Collection, 1990. Cat. No. 181111. The Field Museum, Chicago.

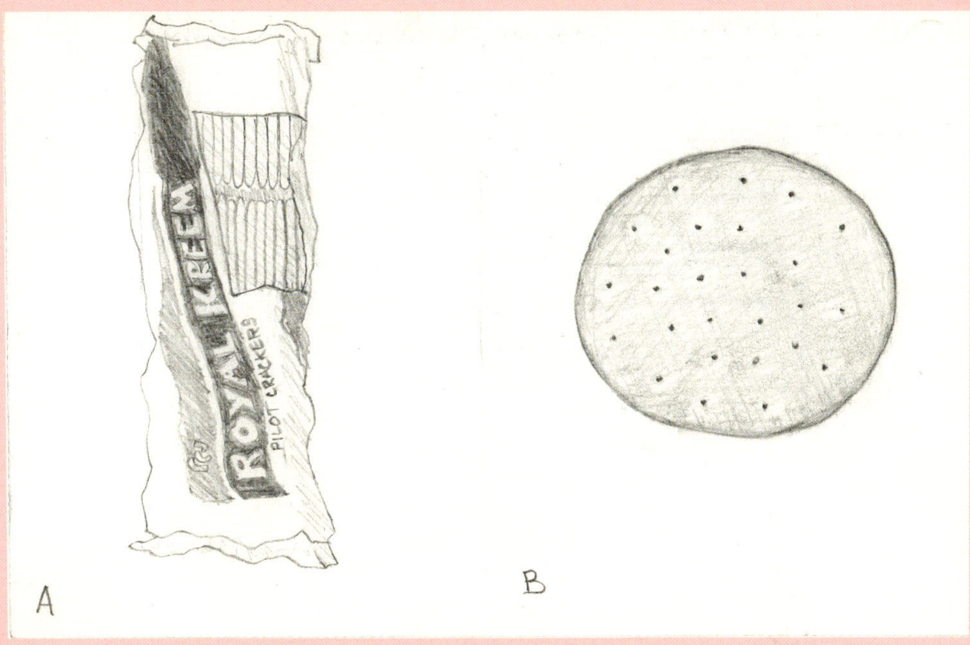

3a: Field Museum Catalogue Card (verso), Nelson Island Seal Party Collection, Accession 3784, *Crackers*, 1990. Cat. No. 181108. The Field Museum, Chicago.

ENT 181108 A–B **Field No.** – **Neg. No.** **Acc.** 3784	**FIELD MUSEUM OF NATURAL HISTORY—ETHNOLOGY** 2-24
	Provenience: Toksook Bay, Nelson Is., Alaska
	People or Culture: Yupik Eskimo
	Object: crackers
	Material: –
	Description: A) "Royal Kreem" pilot crackers (1 pkg. – $14\frac{1}{2}$ oz.) B) large, round soda crackers (6) Used as gift in seal party.
	Dimensions: – (in cm.)
	Collection: Dr. Ann Fienup-Riordan

3b: Field Museum Catalogue Card (recto), Nelson Island Seal Party Collection, Accession 3784, *Crackers*, 1990. Cat. No. 181108. The Field Museum, Chicago.

display, on the recto side, typed information for each Accession 3784 item—and include a pencil rendering of the object. The recto transforms the processed food into "object: tortilla chips" and describes "'Doritos' cool ranch flavor (1 packet – 1 1/8 oz.) Used as gift in seal party"; the verso renders the snack bag in gray two-dimensionality.

The drab cards portray soda crackers, fabric swatches, and assorted matchbooks comprising, along with the Doritos, thirty-eight objects gifted to the Field Museum by Ann Fienup-Riordan, an anthropologist and curator invested in considering both past and present Indigenous potlatches equally for collections (figs. 3a, 3b).[4] Congressional passage of the 1989 charter for a National Museum of the American Indian (NMAI) and the following year's Native American Graves Protection and Repatriation Act (NAGPRA) forced arts institutions receiving federal funds to confront their collections' process in regard to Indigenous communities, past, present, and future. NAGPRA instituted procedures adjudicating the return and restoration of stolen human remains and funerary items, as well as sacred objects and cultural patrimony, to federally recognized tribal nations. At the Field Museum in the 1990s, addressing NAGPRA claims by descendent communities dovetailed with burgeoning conversations around collecting. Acquiring materials from an *uqiquq* (a "seal party" celebrating a Yupik man's first seasonal catch of a bearded seal) or tengmiaqsaraq meant engaging the present practices of Indigenous consumption—in this case items such as instant ramen, toilet paper, and diapers—dismissing these materials as less than "valuable" and "authentic" jewels of Indigenous aesthetic production and exchange. Fienup-Riordan's acquisitions insisted that the Field Museum accept contemporary Indigenous presence in their own homelands by collecting accordingly. To take her perspective, showcasing objects that preserve an Indigenous present should be as desirable as materials that preserved an Indigenous past, and doing so would constitute a significant step for the institution in recognizing the existence of Indigenous communities on their own terms. They too are consumers of banal American foods, here seamlessly integrating these comestibles into continuous Yup'ik traditions. This adaptability belies centuries of US imperatives to cast Indigenous peoples as unable to evolve or change, and thus, with no futurity.

Yet looking at the Field Museum's careful acquisition cards and bagged original items brings to mind courtroom evidence more than museum grandeur. The museum might have updated what was being collected, but its mechanisms to process these items remained unchanged, and the sense of abundance, color, and life—the choice of gifter and giftee existing in the actual celebration—gave way to staid calculation and classification. The accession record assigns value ($35.00 listed on both the accession card and the worksheet); the catalogue cards distance materials from makers or consumers, focusing on "Provenience," "People or Culture," "Object," and "Dimensions." If the originals disappeared, would these details accurately allow for a reconstruction of each item in the collection? How could they, since the catalogue cards omit a detail Fienup-Riordan submitted in her accompanying documentation: "The candy I sent was from the distribution, but the crackers were bought this fall in Anchorage to replace the originals (which my son Nicky ate) and to add flavor [sic] to the collection."[5] Emerging from the juxtaposition of records, then, is the fact that misinterpretation and false narratives are already embedded in what is being acquired and presented as a more modern update, a more "authentic" representation of social practice. "Nicky's" snack attack, ultimately, is the only thing that follows what should have taken place after the tengmiaqsaraq, namely, that the gifted items had a purpose, which was to be consumed by their recipients or transformed into new materials for other social-exchange occasions. The Field Museum's acquisition embalmed an active, continuing process of consumption and renewal through regifting.

Gibson makes these misinterpretations, with a tongue-in-cheek spin, visible in *Acc. 3784*, the wallpaper he designed for the Newberry Library's *Sweet Bitter Love* exhibition. The accession cards can capture neither the feelings, thoughts, or desires of the Yup'ik participants, nor the museum's institutional attempt to stamp these mundane items with unique status that unintentionally produces comical results. With their assertion of seriousness and gravity, the cards and records serve the museum as an "enlightened" accession and miss the point of the junk food representing life's joy and intimacies. The more sober the material record, and its attendant undervaluing of this collection, the more ridiculous the effect. Jeffrey Gibson, as his wallpaper demonstrates, understands both the absurdity and the humor. His wallpaper repositions selected drawings from the cards in a repeat pattern against an ombré background reminiscent of a sunrise or a sunset, which has the effect of making the items both individual and dynamic. Each drawing has a palette that underscores that this work is neither still life nor verisimilitude—a white diaper, opened and looking both like a puzzle piece and a crucifix, joins a cyan-red instant ramen container, a fully turquoise bar of Ivory soap, an atomic-orange bag of Doritos—rather than restoring the original colors of the objects to the technical renderings. The pattern repetition is harmonizing and invites the viewer to contemplate the ways in which members of the Nelson Island community, or anyone, exchanging these otherwise-ordinary items might view the object of one's desire. This isn't a dour, gray-washed world of ethnography where understanding Indigeneity is limited to a colonial dating system and scholarly projection that set the boundaries of authenticity firmly in the past. This is the immediate and playful survivance and futurity that is contemporary Indigeneity, part pop-art, part innovative Indigenous modernism, and part history.[6]

Gibson's wallpaper and paintings began as site-specific works shown in a collaboration between the Smart Museum at the University of Chicago and Chicago's Newberry Library, providing an aesthetic and cultural rebuke to the "portraits" of Indigenous individuals painted by Anglo-American artist Elbridge Ayer (E. A.) Burbank in the late nineteenth century and held at the Newberry Library. "These aren't pictures of our ancestors," Jeffrey Gibson noted, when reflecting on Burbank's portraits of individuals like Pretty Eagle and Pahl-Lee. "They aren't even our ancestors."[7] Burbank's claim to relevance rested not on his skill and genius as an artist (he was a passable portraitist at best) but on adjudicating and commodifying "real" Indian leaders for audiences, like George Catlin or photographer Edward Curtis (Burbank's contemporary), and reinforcing Indigenous disappearance by using blank backgrounds and inscrutable expressions to conjure the quintessential "the last of" trope.[8] Portrayals such as Burbank's influenced erroneous concepts of Indigenous "authenticity," so Gibson dispenses with Burbank by instead putting forth Indigenous-led relationships and alternate futurities. Arrayed along one wall of the Newberry's Hanson Gallery, the original Field Museum catalogue card drawings, accompanied by facsimiles to show the catalogue information on the obverse of the cards, sat in glass cases below the Burbank paintings, to mediate Gibson's preference for displaying the images informing his work (the original drawings) and the Field Museum's desire to demonstrate the documentation displayed in text. The cards faced Gibson's newly commissioned mixed-media works, which incorporate material culture Gibson collects. Here tension—literally the past facing off with the present and the visual imperatives of an individual juxtaposed with those of an institution—is transformed by Gibson into possibility that offers both agony and ecstasy, as the title *Sweet Bitter Love*, drawn from a Roberta Flack song of the same name, suggests (see page 13). Gibson does not waste time engaging in visual dialogue with Burbank, because doing so would validate Burbank's proposition that he offers authentic representations to viewers. Instead, Gibson leans into the disruptive possibilities; he offers alternative modes to depict these individuals and surrounds Burbank with Indigenous community and context, with *Acc. 3784* wallpaper and his own portraits. The wallpaper is an unexpected backdrop in so "traditional" a space as the Newberry, and the Burbank portraits cease to be foci as a result. Instead, this is wallpaper as point of entry into Gibson's considerations about what and when institutions acquire, the limitations of well-known narrative, and the unexplored possibilities within these places. Both amulet and map, the wallpaper is where Gibson manifests altered interpretations and understandings of both collection and acquisition practices.

Space and time considerations unite themes in Gibson's two Chicago exhibitions. Spatial dynamics also act as through lines that help us to understand how Gibson's works remake the contexts around them and allow viewers to bring new questions to the locations where these works are held, where they are displayed, what they are reacting to, and are also inspired by. Gibson's raw footage of the

Marquette Building, like the *Acc. 3784* wallpaper's relationship to the Field Museum, offers suggestions of how to walk differently through Chicago space. Starting on the contemporary street, Gibson's video footage emphasizes the transition from urban light to darkened space. In the mid-twentieth century, modernization "upgrades" of the Marquette Building altered the interior in a way that removed the natural sources of light that existed in the original design, thereby "processing" the building like the plastic-enclosed bag of Doritos at the Field Museum. Today, the polished stone, Tiffany glass murals, and bronze elevator banks must rely heavily on the artificial (in this case, illumination) to continue to project their artistic presence and pride of place. Gibson's criticism regarding Newberry's Burbank "portraits" of Indigenous individuals comes to mind as the camera slowly pans around the Marquette lobby's representations of "Indians." As he notes, the mosaics and interior bronze bas-reliefs created by Amy Aldis Bradley, Jacob Holzer, Edward Kemeys, and Louis Tiffany "don't deliver on what a portrait claims to deliver and be able to do. It is a representation of a historical moment [the encounter between sovereign Indigenous communities and the representatives of ancien régime France], a gaze, a circumstance, but it's not an accurate representation of the individual it claims to be."[9] The iconographic program is as fictional as that of Burbank, who was a rough contemporary of the Marquette Building's artists, saying more about the general ability of the United States and Canada to process Indigenous individuals in the 1890s than seventeenth-century historical accuracy. Surrounding Tiffany and Holzer's mosaic elegy to Marquette—a technicolor rendering of the exterior friezes—are eleven elevator banks on the ground floor and mezzanine, each topped with a bas-relief depicting different Indigenous leaders, French priests, colonial officials, and voyageurs (fur traders) (fig. 4).[10] Lit from below and positioned directly above rectangular elevator doors, the reliefs uncannily resemble the image of Han Solo frozen in carbonite and hanging in an intergalactic smuggler's palace. Marquette, dead center on the first floor, is the lone relief who looks youthful and receives, along with his name, the additional context of being an "explorer, voyager, missionary" and having "discovered the Chicago River." This assertion seems

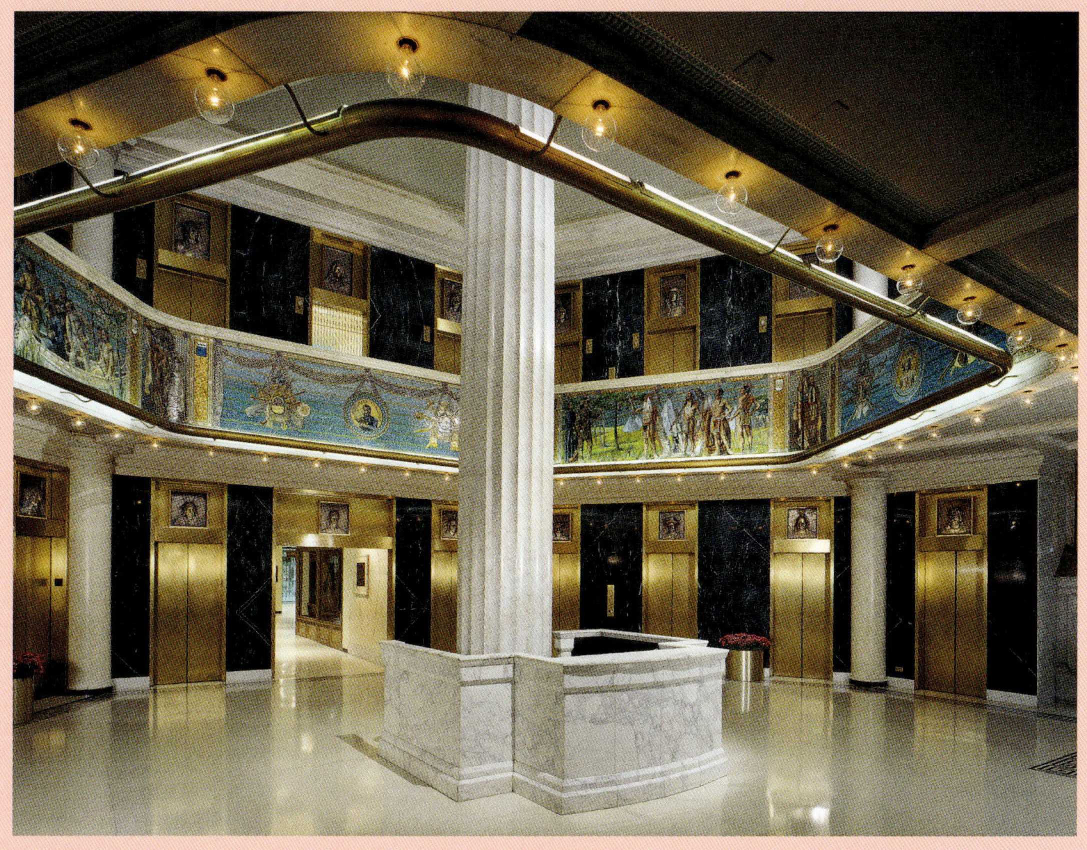

4: Glass mosaic frieze in the rotunda of the Marquette Building, Chicago. Designed by J. A. Holler, 1895.

amusingly misguided if one looks immediately to the right and sees . . . Chicagou, whose name immediately suggests otherwise (though this is not the source of the city's name). As part of an Indigenous delegation in 1725, Šikaakwa (Chicagou) met with Louis XV at Versailles and received gifts from the king and nobles that he brought back home to Kaskaskia.[11] The omission of this history, despite meticulously recorded Jesuit accounts, and the assignment of discovery to "Marquette" in North America, rather than to "Chicagou" discovering Europe, reinforces Gibson's point of view about representation. Gibson's video work with the Marquette Building may be unfinished, but those who have seen his wallpaper, paintings, and sculptures can walk through the space marked by the work he has created, reframing this architecture and inviting a fresh response for himself and for viewers.

As a MacArthur Fellow, "I'm in a relationship to the building in that I am a beneficiary of what happens here," Gibson explains, adding that his videos in the Marquette Building were prepared not for engagement with the decoration for which it is famous but rather, for "the people of color who have to exist within [the building] . . . who are there out of need and employment."[12] His observation challenges Marquette's famed decorations as worthy objects of veneration. The concept animating the videos was to bring the Marquette Building's security and environmental staff to the fore, homing in on other optics, wrenching us into a reconsideration of the things that are processing us, and making evident the Marquette Building as a point in time more complex than adoration or revulsion alone. Though incomplete, the videos invite contrast between Gibson's own art, and his masterful embraces of shine, ornament, adornment, and radiant color, with the harrowing lobby space. "Indigenous kinship philosophies try to equate nature as an equal, and how do we speak or engage with it [then]?" Gibson speculates. His question serves as a reminder that the building's iconography values only Chicago's human actors, forgetting the ecological roots of the city, evident in Chicago's very name, versions of which translate as '"the place of wild garlic" (or "onion") in several Algonquian languages.[13] Watching the video as it passes through the near-empty lobby and mezzanine, he remarks, "The use of natural stone and marble [in Marquette] as representative

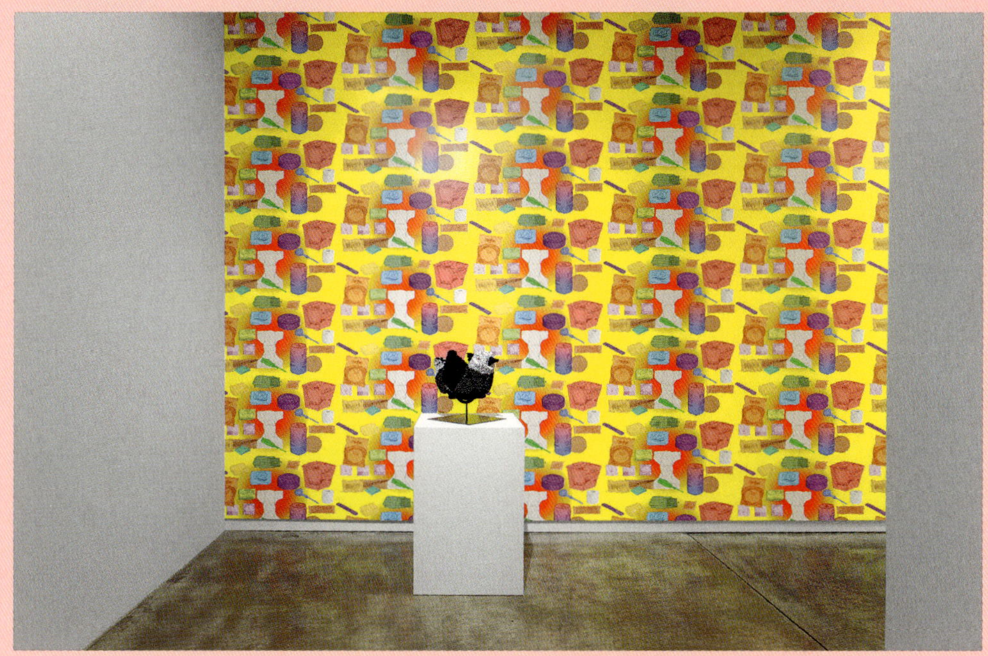

5: *Black Beauty* in front of *Acc. 3784* wallpaper. Installation view, *Beyond the Horizon*, Kavi Gupta, Chicago, November 13, 2021–January 8, 2022.

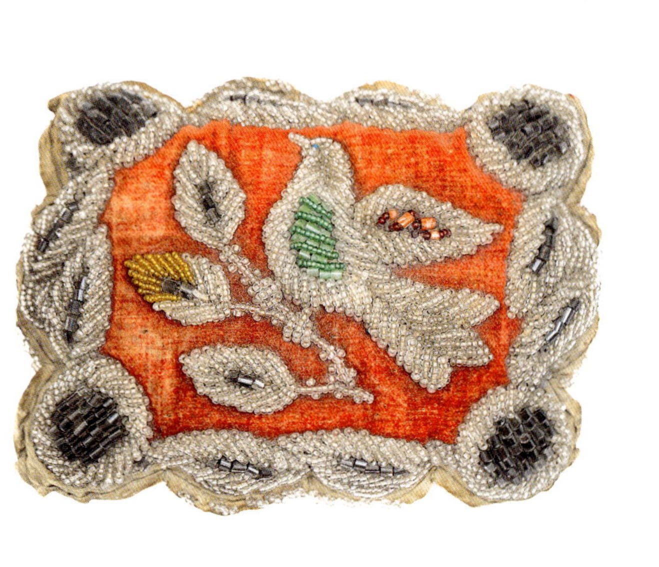

6: Beaded whimsey, circa 1900s (artist unknown). Velvet, cotton fabric, glass beads, cotton thread, and cedar pulp. 6 1/2 x 8 /12 x 4 inches (16.5 x 21.6 x 10.2 cm). From Jeffrey Gibson's collection.

of [geologic] time—this kind of use of stone [in the lobby] is forcing something to do what you want it to do … it's totally aggressive harnessing of space."[14]

The black-and-white marble floor mosaics of the Marquette lobby and mezzanine, bordered with Greek key patterns and Marquette's cross, seem flat and dull when contrasted with Gibson's "Black Beauty" bird sculpture—the first thing visitors to *Beyond the Horizon* see in front of a field of the *Acc. 3784* wallpaper. Rounded, weighty, and three-dimensional, the black-and-white bird is "a design form … a transitional image that can speak to non-Indigenous and Indigenous"[15] (figs. 5, 6). The bird makes no claim on verisimilitude, unlike the attempt by the Marquette Building décor to project "truth," and therein lies the bird's power. The birds, like the rounded elements Gibson introduced into his portraits and the quilt-block paintings in *Beyond the Horizon*, are inspired by and drawn from beaded whimsies, barrettes, bags. Created for both powwow participants and regulars, as well as for sale to tourists, these objects have as ornate and diverse a decorative program as the Marquette Building and are also traditions dating back to the nineteenth century. Yet unlike the Marquette Building, they do not impose their process or their interpretation onto viewers, and instead embrace an aesthetic that speaks to multiple interests. Gibson's inspiration in these special, but everyday, flights of material fancy effectively demolishes the idea that the decorative purpose of the Marquette Building is what artists, and viewers, aspire to.

Beyond the Horizon is an apt title for a show encompassing the portraits from the Newberry and two sculptures. These works return to and expand on artistic practices Gibson first began in the early 2000s, alongside new quilt-block paintings that integrate Indigenous whimsies and vintage Indigenous images. The *Acc. 3784* wallpaper features prominently, but now it welcomes Gibson's portraits first displayed at the Newberry. The effect and contrast are immediate and electric. *Sweet Bitter Love* and *Acc. 3784* powerfully changed the context of Burbank's canvases, but conserving Burbank's portraits (as well as the Field Musuem catalogue cards) required dim lighting in the exhibition space. Now fully illuminated at Kavi Gupta, the *Acc. 3784* wallpaper crackles with vivid power, liberated from its former task of muting Burbank's settler imperatives and preventing Burbank from continuing to cast his cultural spell through mimetic reproduction of the outward features of his portrait subjects. Complementing Gibson's portraits, the wallpaper—and its position in proximity to the dynamic and colorful quilt-block paintings—suggests that these images are forming a new wallpaper of their own. The whole effect prompts us to look, to look again, and to continue to process seemingly disparate information that comes together as harmonious whole. As Gibson puts it, these works are "to sit together, intersect, and be in dialogue—and become a different type of narrative." *Beyond the Horizon*, as he explains, is the title of a gospel song, and these walls indeed reflect his aspiration "that you have faith that you have a future beyond where we are today."[16]

Seen in the afterglow of *Sweet Bitter Love*, and now in *Beyond the Horizon*, the Marquette Building, like Burbank, emerges as the antithesis of the animated promise of things to come and the enticing myriad relationships manifested in Gibson's wallpaper and quilt-block paintings. In this book, *Acc. 3784* transforms from wallpaper to endpaper, moving like a trickster character from a gray-and-white penciled card, destined for obscurity, to technicolor walls, and now, forming a protective lining that envelops Jeffrey Gibson's, rather than Burbank's or Marquette's, projects. Wallpaper by its very nature is a consumable, processed good, like the materials depicted in and upon it. The design's ability to take on multiple lives, changing place and format, reanimates the cycle denied the Field Museum's Diet Pepsi and instant ramen, which should have been consumed, and the fabric swatches that ought to have been made into a quilt to be gifted anew at a future Yup'ik social event tradition. Today it is fashionable to say that we all want to be part of nature. But Jeffrey Gibson's wallpaper and its celebration of the Yup'ik tengmiaqsaraq continuation and futurity showcase that in an Indigenous worldview, processing is part of nature.

    The highest goal for processed food manufacturers is to achieve the "bliss point," the industry term that expresses the delightful, yet ephemeral, sensation on one's tastebuds that leaves the consumer craving more.[17] Jeffrey Gibson's wallpaper, like his evolving work, takes on what processing is about, which is finding our bliss point, that element of appeal to a certain taste that evokes a certain craving for more processing, not less. It appeals to greater recognition of different ways of being, rather than their erasure or their shelving. The entry of these everyday items, with their assumption of spiritual significance, into the Field Museum arrests that cycle. Driven by the paramount consideration of preservation, the museum has erroneously attempted to extend the shelf life of precious moments that are meant to be parts of a flowing time-space continuum. The items of the 1990 Yup'ik tengmiaqsaraq are not representative of inauthenticity—they are the common goods of *that* moment and showcase an acceptance of processing as a key component in life. The actual items remain trapped by the museum's conservation, and the cards reflect neither the joy of giving away mundane objects nor the intangible social impact of the delight each item gives in return. Ultimately, Indigenous-made whimsies, or Doritos at a Yup'ik seal party, are facets of an incredibly varied, ever-changing authenticity that Burbank, and the Marquette Building, and even the Field Museum's accession procedures, attempted to sublimate and replace with a canned, or rather, processed narrative that firmly located Indigenous peoples in the past. In each case, people are circumscribed until all of the fanciful, undignified, messy, silly, ephemeral, trivial things about a person— the very things that make us human and individual—are made to live outside the official record. In *Sweet Bitter Love* and *Beyond the Horizon*, Jeffrey Gibson denies the approach taken by the Field Museum and the Marquette Building as the only, or the most consequential, ways to process Indigenous experience, then and now. He shares with us works that update the manner of processing these American experiences, making visible in his portraits, wallpaper, and sculptures that which institutions in the service of "preserving" the past have adulterated, like chemicals in food.

◖OTES

1   Chicago sits in the homelands of the Anishinaabeg, or Neshnabek, comprising the Odawa, Ojibwe, and Potawatomi [Bodéwadmi] nations in a confederation known as the Three Fires Council, along with several other Indigenous nations.

2   Ann Fienup-Riordan, "Documentation for Nelson Island Seal Party Collection," notes included in Accession Record 3784, December 6, 1990, Field Museum of Natural History, Chicago (Fienup-Riordan's italics). According to Field Museum documentation, "A seal party (*uqiquq*) is usually given to celebrate a man's first *tungunquq* (bearded seal) of the season. This particular party, although designated *uqiquq*, was given to celebrate a five-year-old boy's first little bird (*tengmiaqsaraq*), which he had caught and killed with his hands." Ann Fienup-Riordan, notes included in "Documentation for Nelson Island Seal Party Collection," June 23, 1998, the Field Museum of Natural History (Fienup-Riordan's italics).

3   Jeffrey Gibson, in conversation with the author, Gibson's studio, Claverack, New York, December 20, 2021 (hereafter "Gibson, conversation with the author, December 20, 2021").

4   Ann Fienup-Riordan, *Eskimo Essays: Yup'ik Lives and How We See Them* (New Brunswick, NJ: Rutgers University Press, 1990, 2003), 37–48; Fienup-Jordan, "Documentation for Nelson Island Seal Party Collection," notes, June 23, 1990, Field Museum.

5   Fienup-Jordan, "Documentation for Nelson Island Seal Party Collection," notes, June 23, 1990, Field Museum.

6   On modernism and Indigeneity, Philip Deloria, *Becoming Mary Sully: Toward an American Indian Abstract* (Seattle: University of Washington Press, 2019).

7   Jeffrey Gibson, in conversation with the author, Gibson's Studio, Claverack, New York, August 18, 2021.

8   See also Abigail Winograd, "Beading for Boneta, a Gift for Pahl Lee: Jeffrey Gibson's Tessellated Histories," in this volume; Jean M. O'Brien, *Firsting and Lasting: Writing Indians out of Existence in New England* (Minneapolis: University of Minnesota Press, 2010).

9   Gibson, conversation with the author, December 20, 2021

10   First-floor elevator relief
representations are identified as
"De Manthet; Big Snake; Jolliet;
Talon; Noon Day; Marquette;
Chicagou; Little Panther;
Tonty; Shaubena; La Taupine."
On the Marquette Building's
mezzanine, the names read
"Waubonsie (Potowatomi
leader); Hairy Bear; Fontenac
[sic]; War Eagle; Nika; La Salle;
Chassagoac; Brown Moose; De
L'Hut; Black Hawk; Keokuk."

11   *The Jesuit Relations and
Allied Documents: Travels
and Explorations of the Jesuit
Missionaries in North America
(1610–1791), with introduction
by Reuben Gold Thwaites*
(Cleveland: Burrows Brothers,
1896; repr. New York: Albert &
Charles Boni, 1925), 426–28.

12   Gibson, conversation with the
author, December 20, 2021.

13   The name Chicago is derived
from the names that many
different Algonquin-speaking
people gave to the place. For
example, in Myaamia, the
word is šikaakonki, while in
Bodwewadmi the word is
Zhekagoynak. Each one has a
slightly different meaning, but
most of them translate to some
version of place of wild onions,
garlic, skunk, or something else
with a strong smell.

14   On Chicago name: John F.
Swenson, "Chicagoua/Chicago:
The Origin, Meaning, and
Etymology of a Place Name,"
Illinois Historical Journal 84,
no. 4 (Winter 1991): 235; Gibson,
conversation with the author,
December 20, 2021.

15   Gibson, conversation with the
author, December 20, 2021.

16   Gibson, conversation with the
author, December 20, 2021.

17   Michael Moss, "The
Extraordinary Science
of Addictive Junk Food,"
New York Times, February
20, 2013; Michael Moss, *Salt,
Sugar, Fat: How the Food
Giants Hooked Us* (New York:
Random House, 2013).

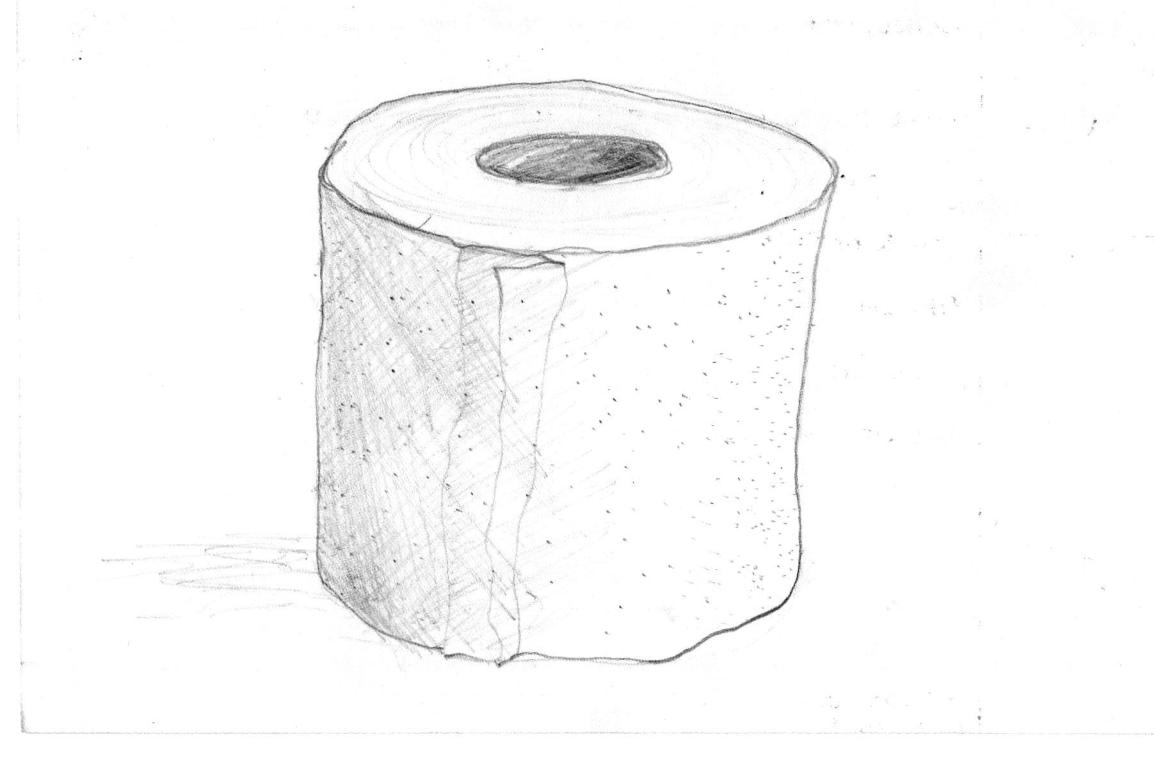

FIELD MUSEUM OF NATURAL HISTORY—ETHNOLOGY   2-22

Provenience: Toksook Bay, Nelson Is., Alaska

People or Culture: Yupik Eskimo

Object: toilet paper

Material: —

Description: white (1 roll).

Used as gift in seal party.

Dimensions: —
(in cm.)

Collection: Dr. Ann Fienup-Riordan

BEYOND THE HORIZON

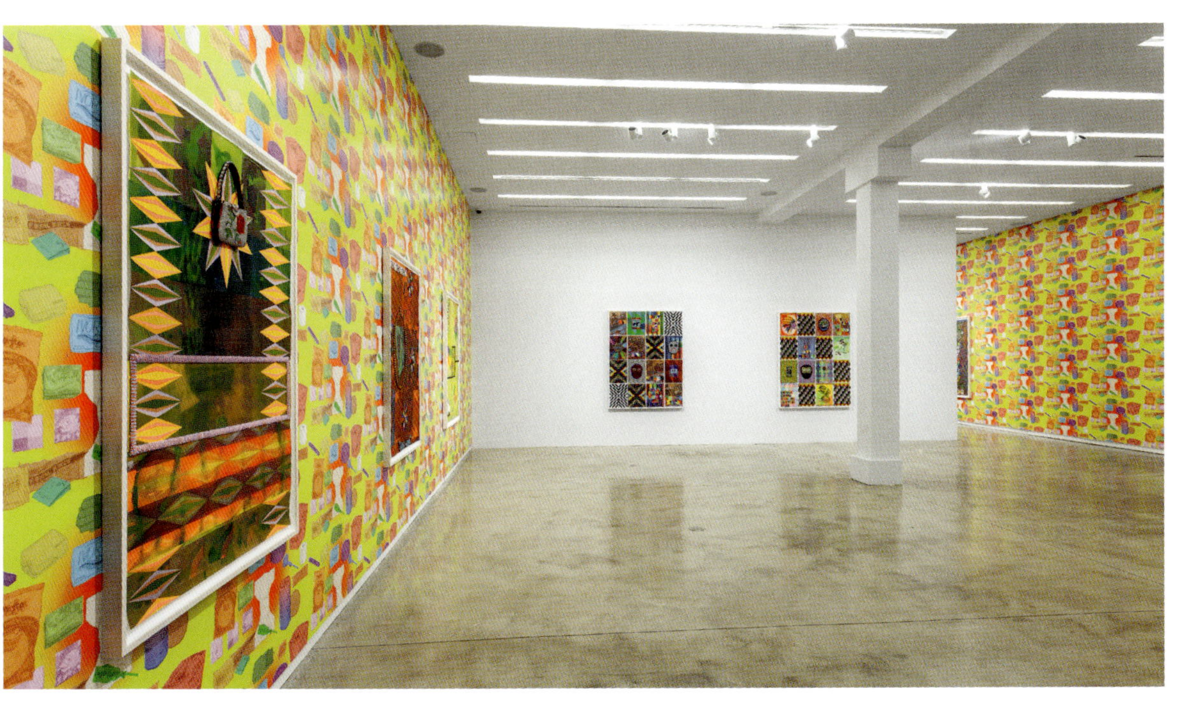

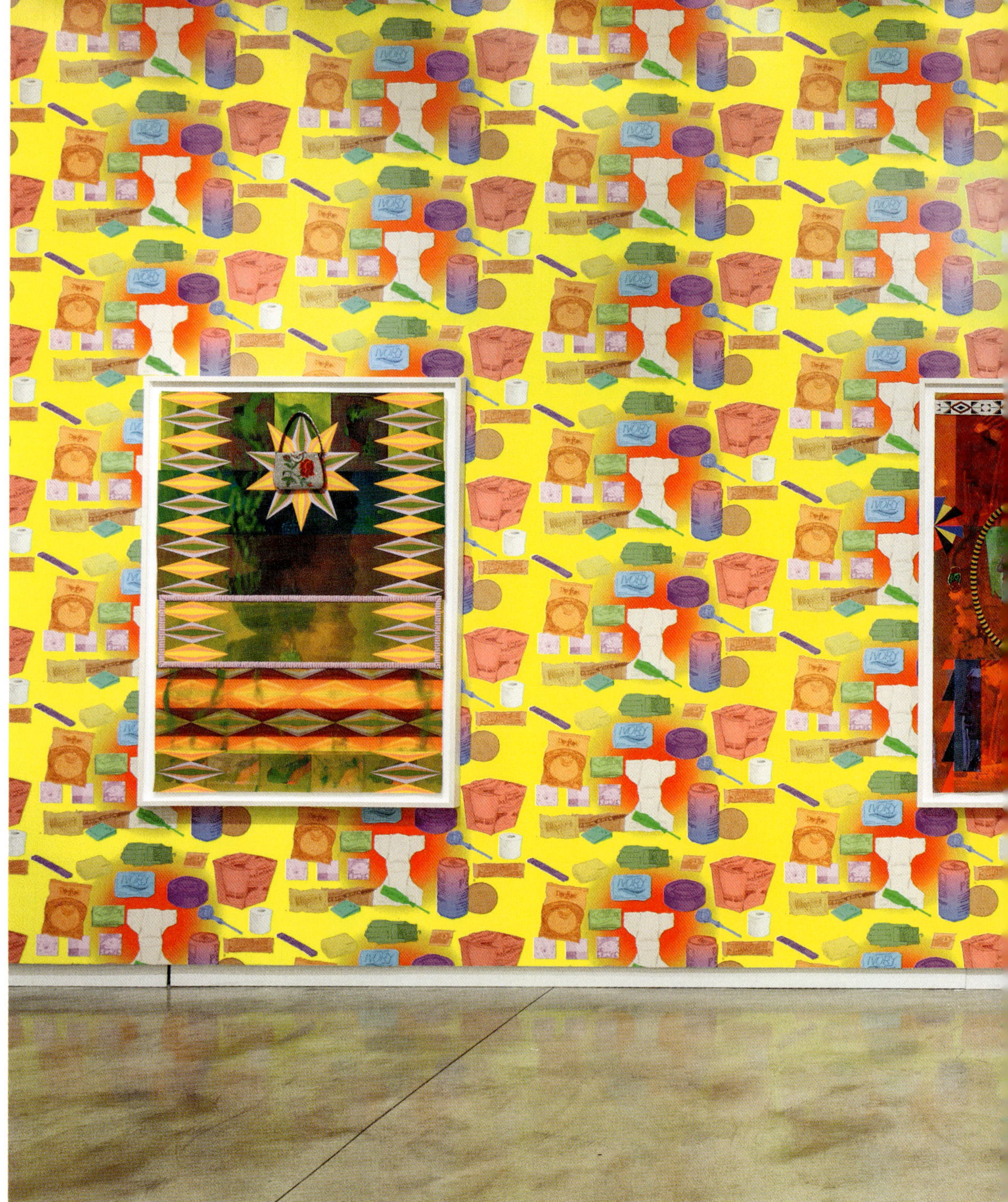

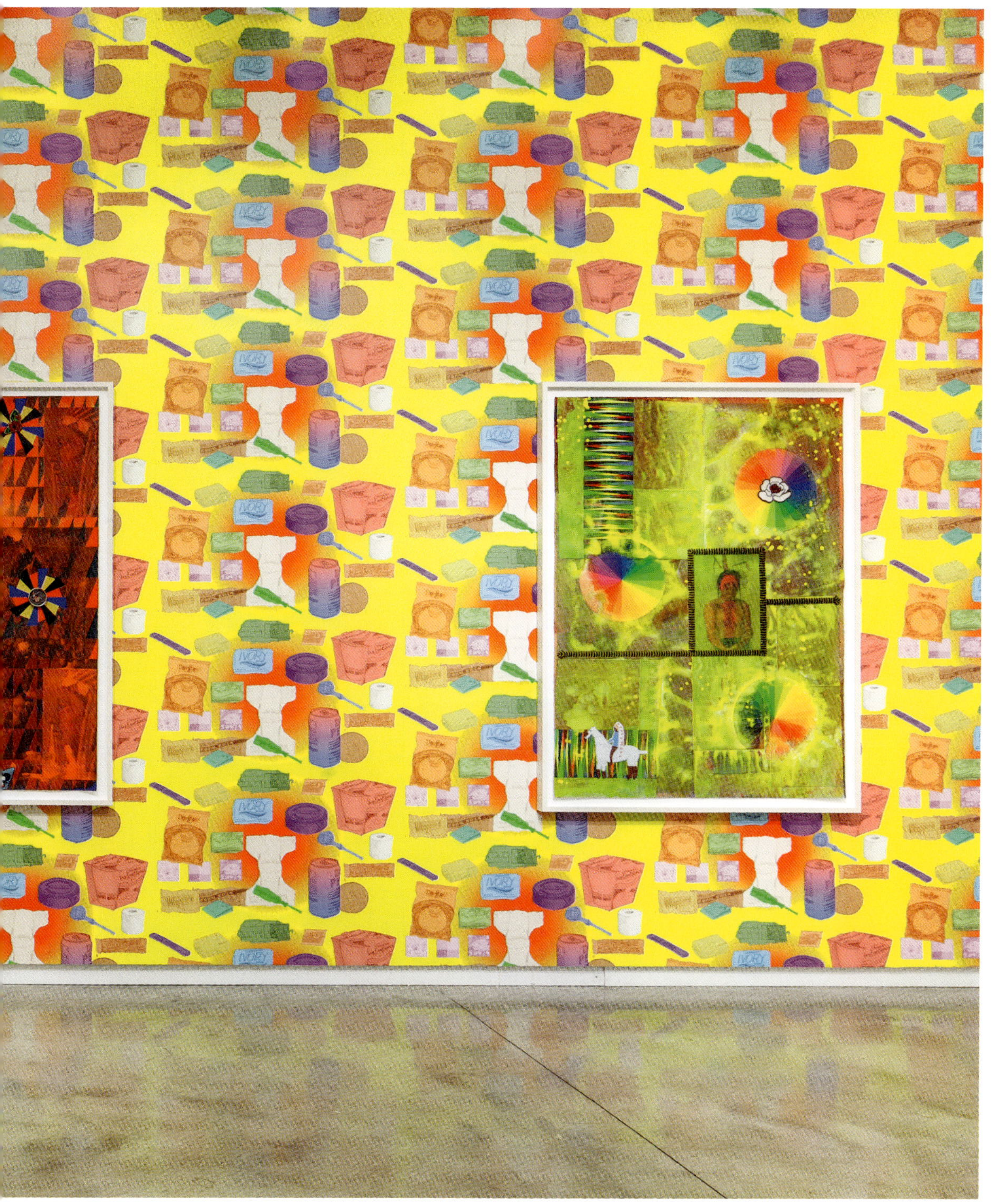

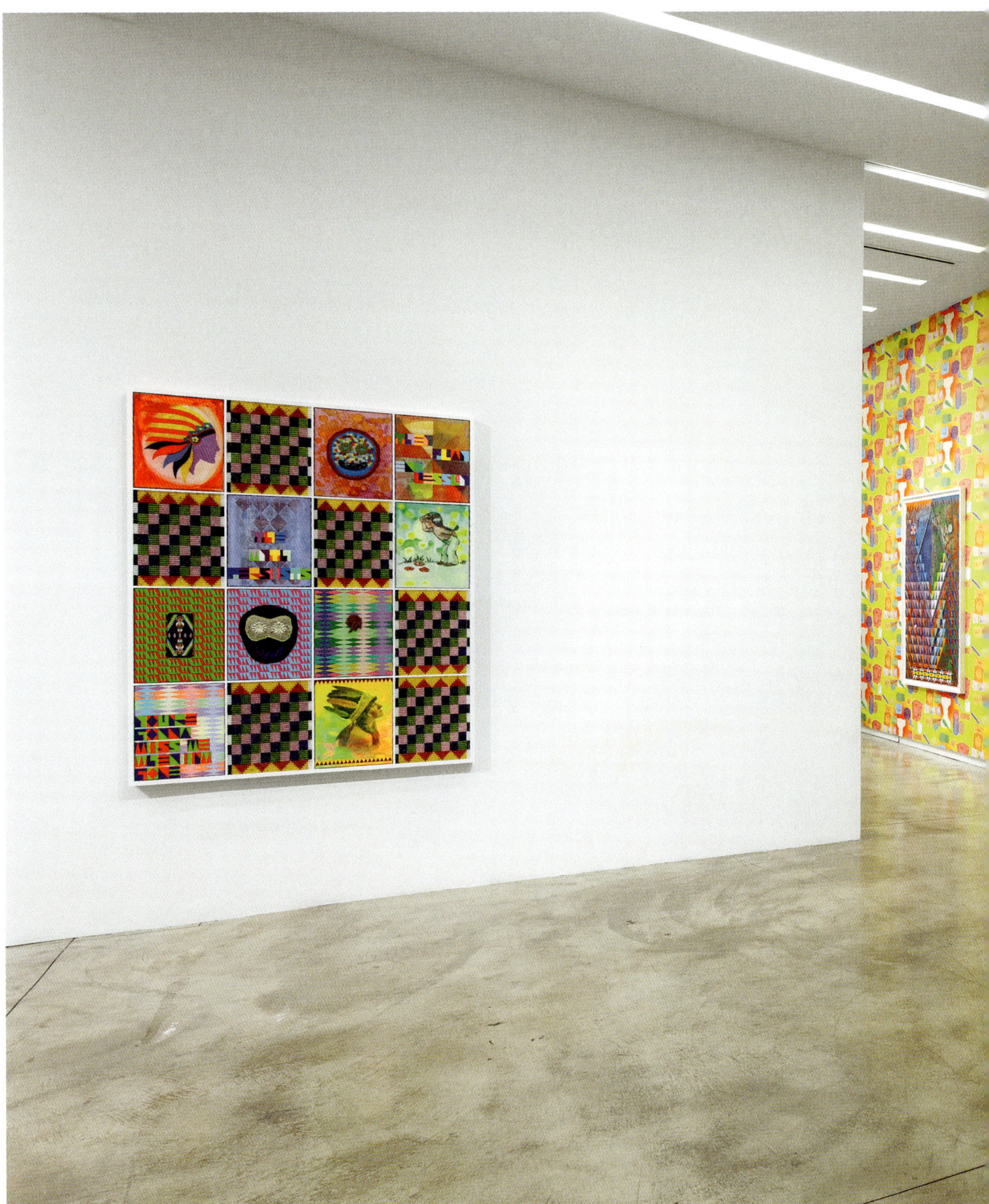

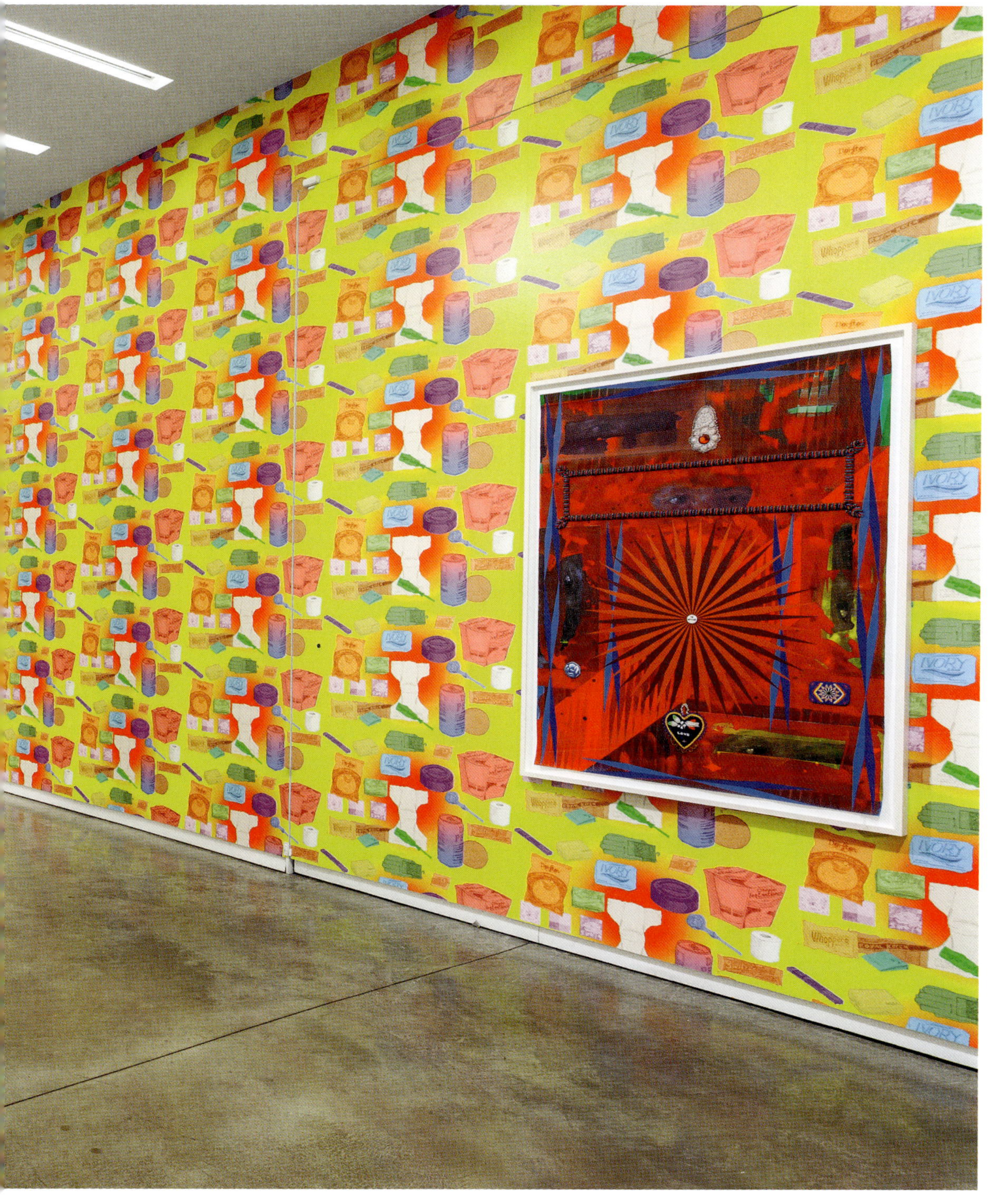

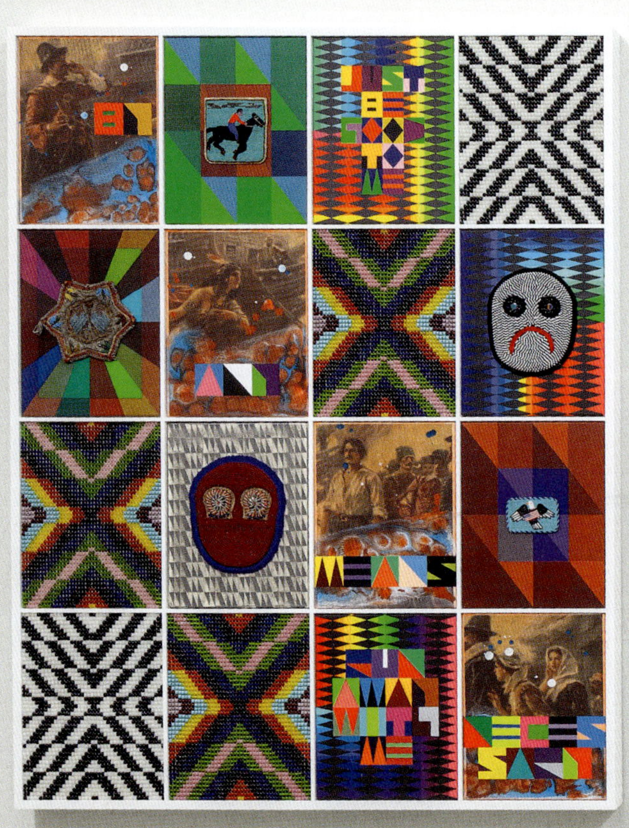

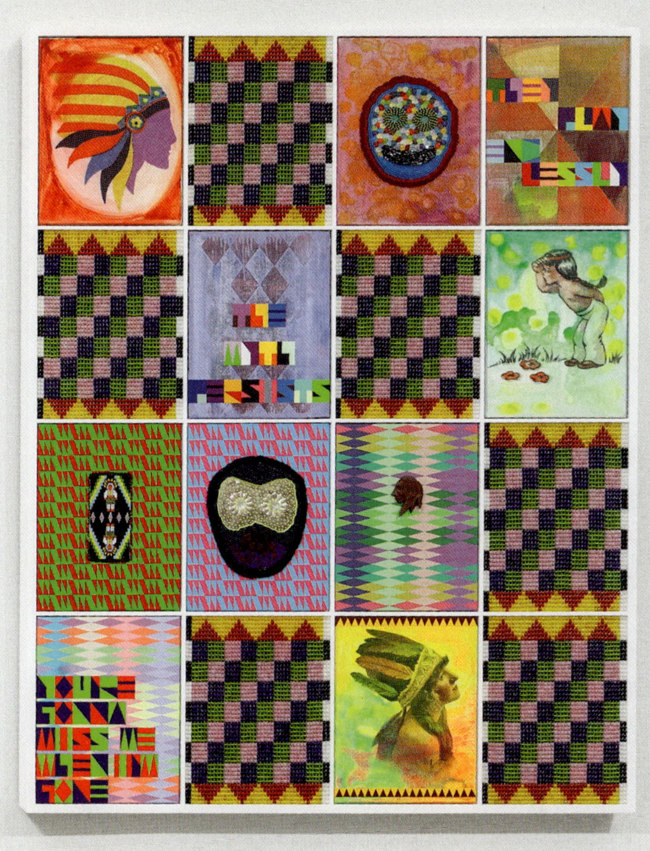

THEY
PLAY
END
LESSLY

THE
MYTH
PERSISTS

YOURE
GONNA
MISS ME
WHEN IM
GONE

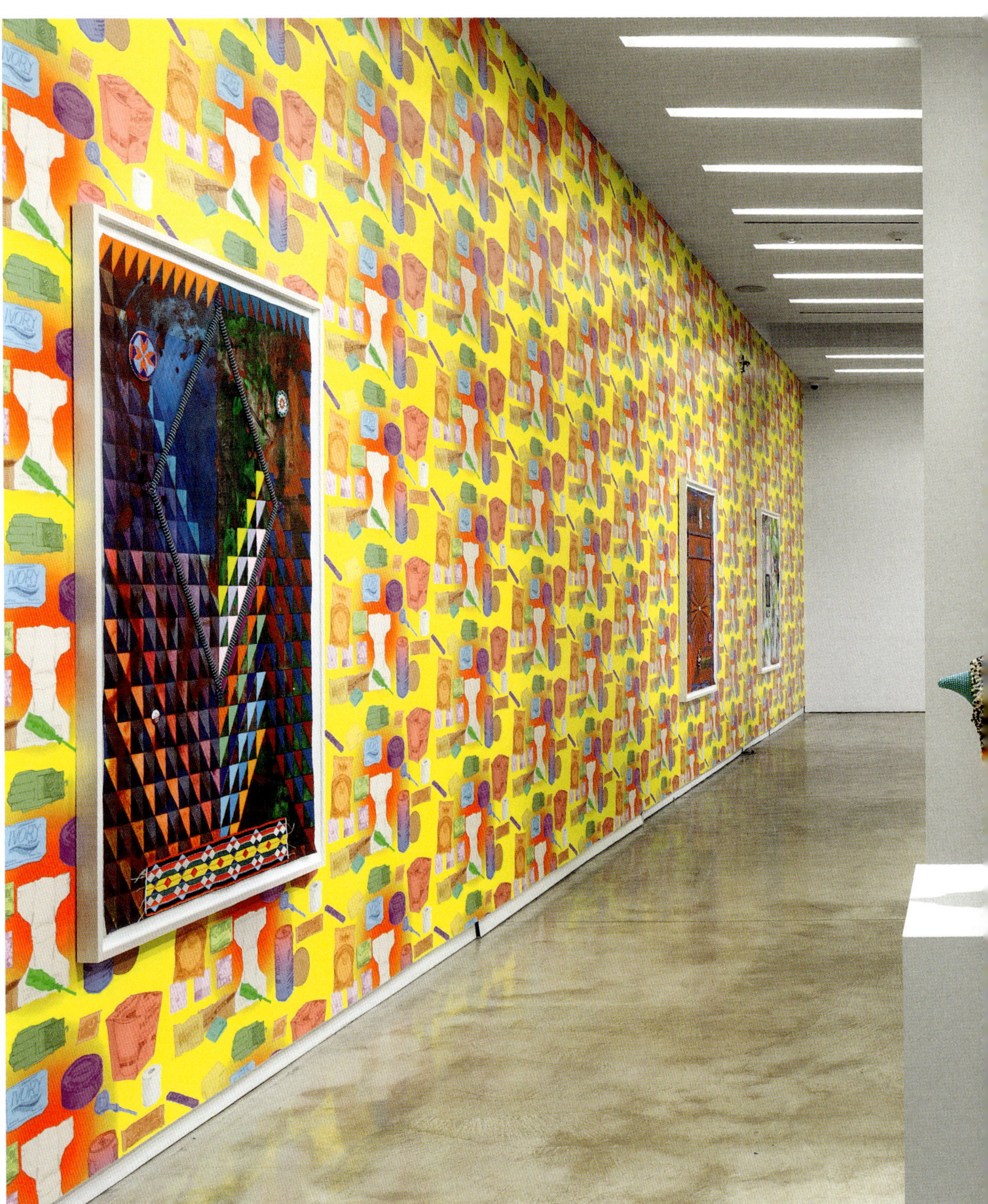

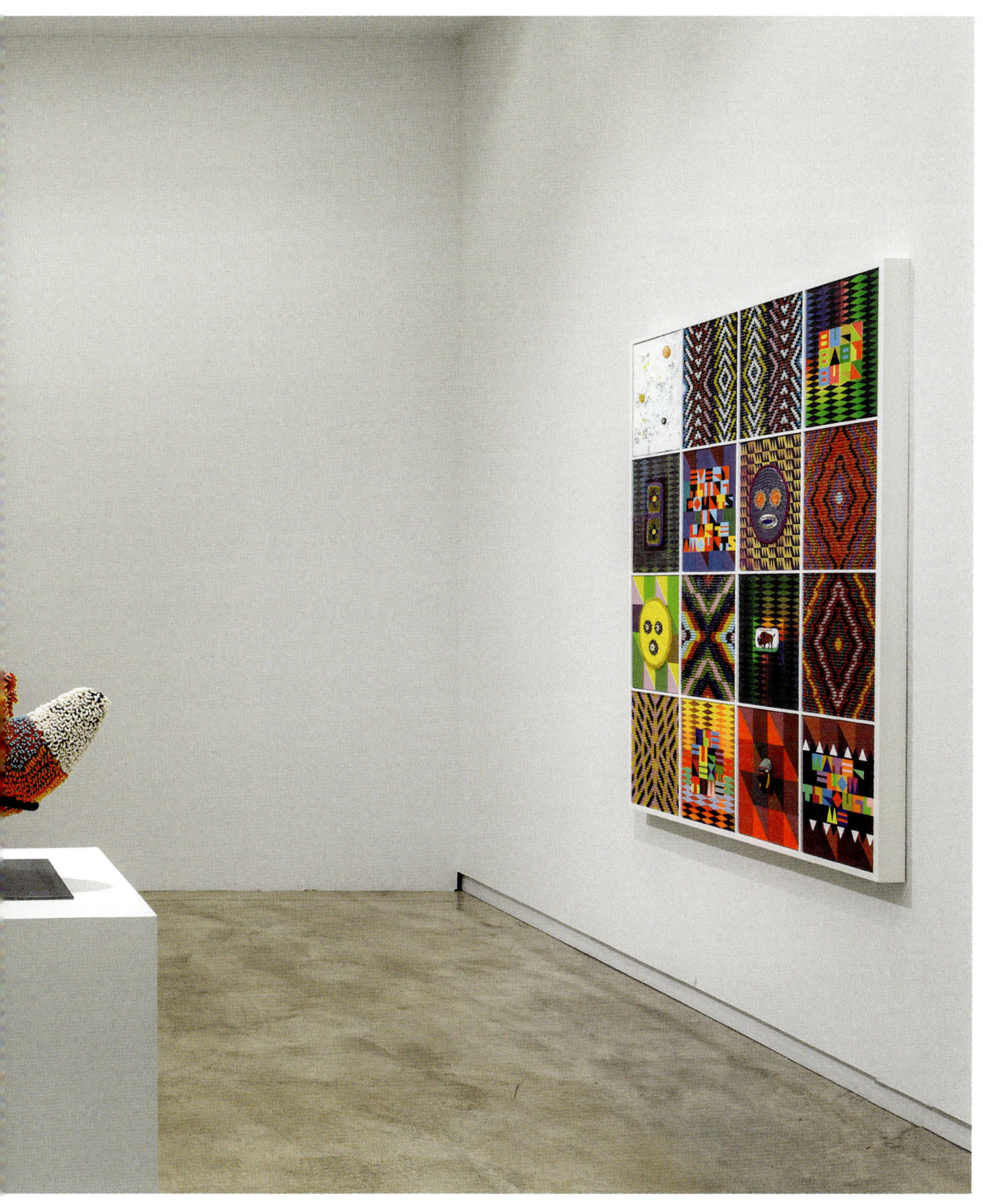

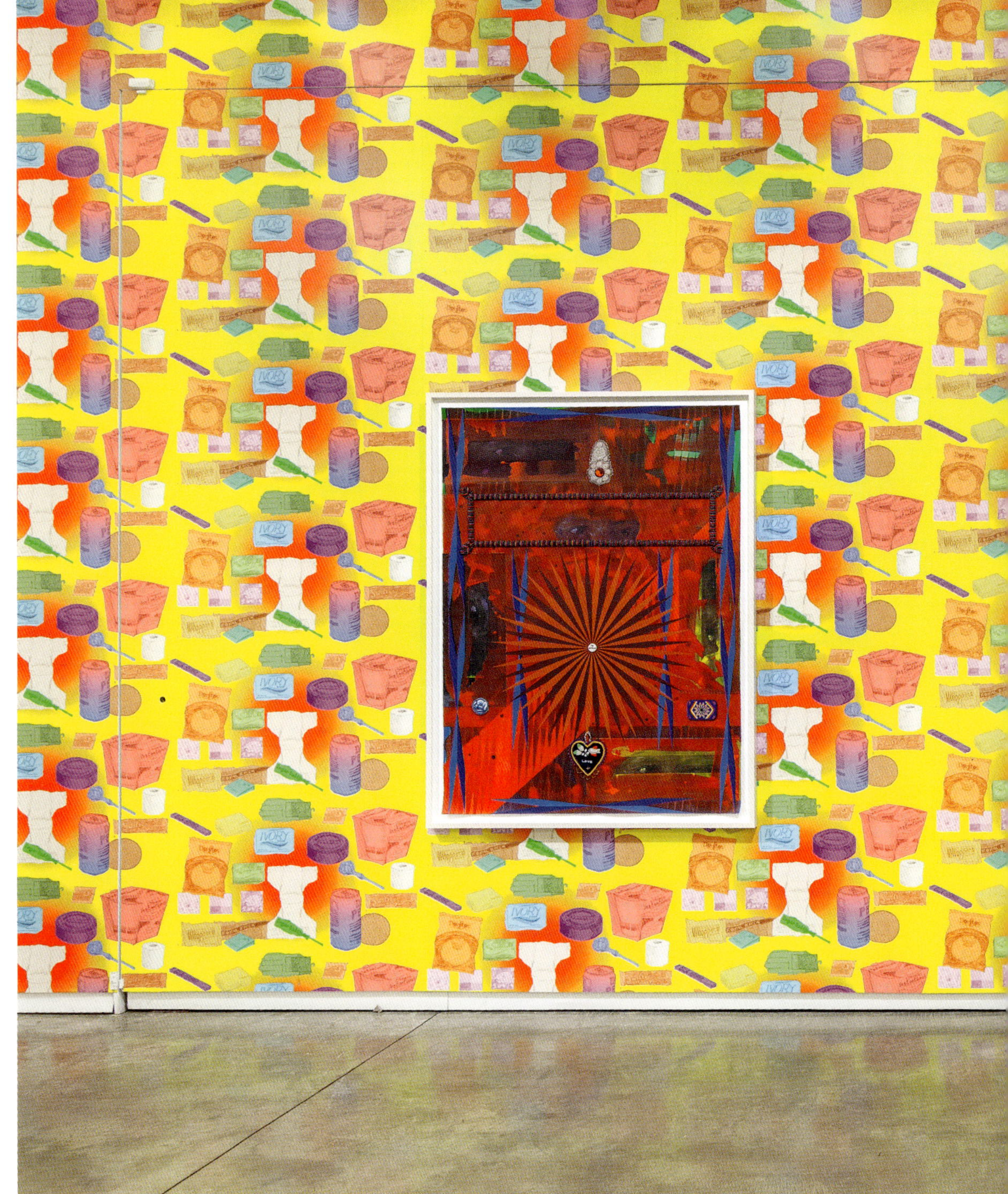

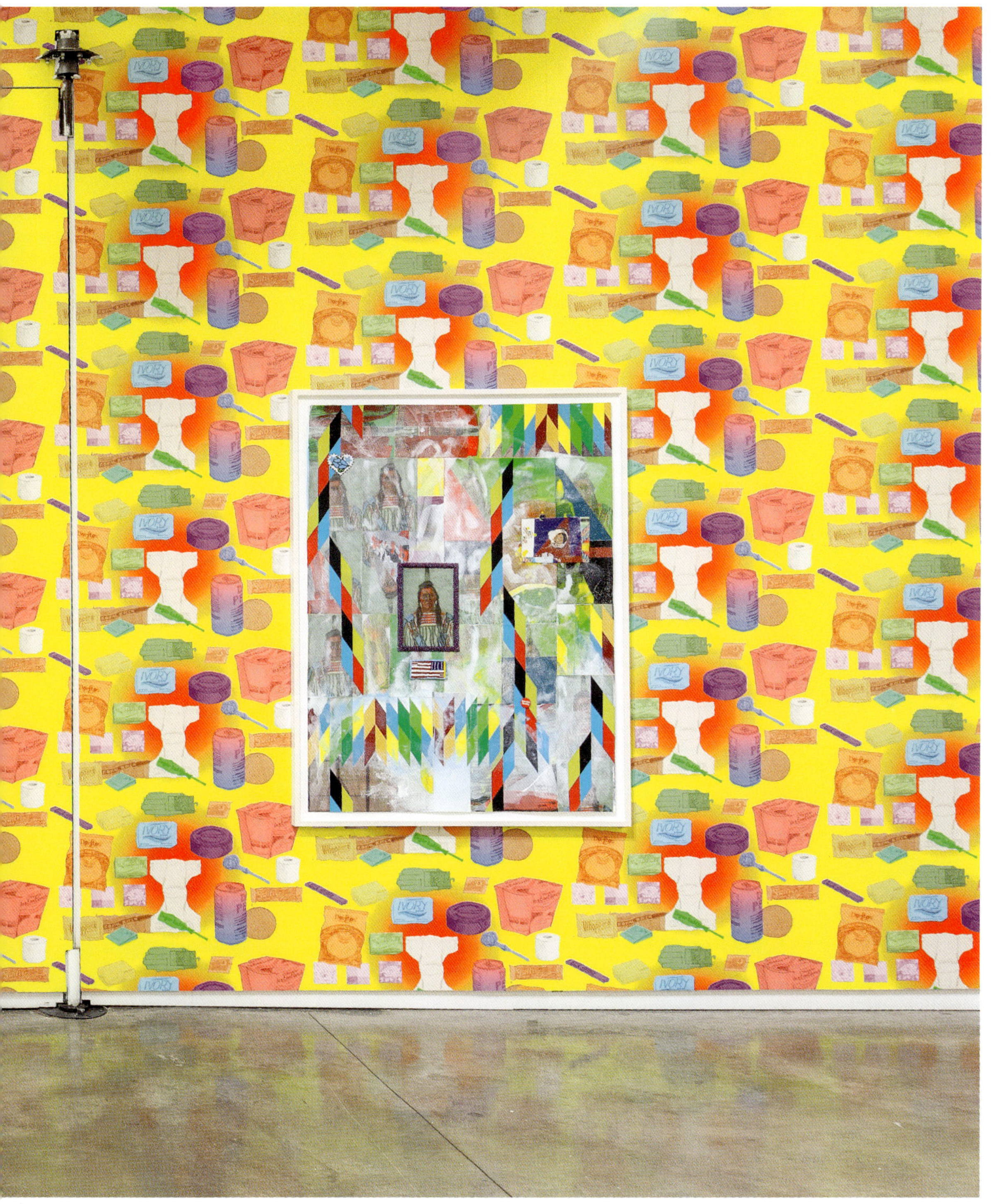

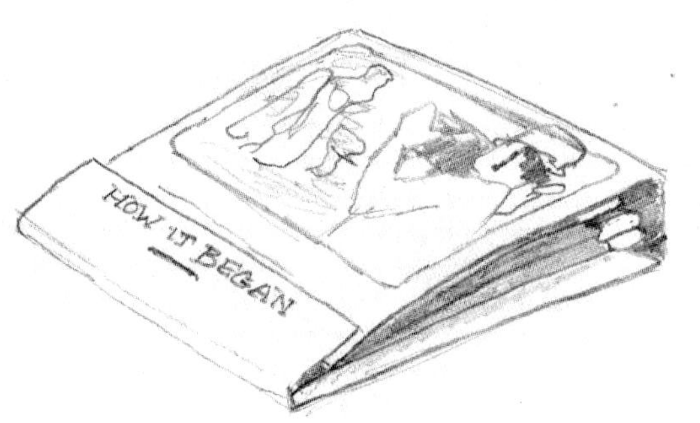
HOW IT BEGAN

FIELD MUSEUM OF NATURAL HISTORY—ETHNOLOGY   2-22

Field No. –	**Provenience:** Toksook Bay, Nelson Is., Alaska **People or Culture:** Yupik Eskimo **Object:** matches **Material:** – **Description:** "Diamond" – <u>Mother's Day</u> (1 book), <u>The Airplane</u> (1 book), <u>The Box Camera</u> (2 books). Used as gift in seal party.
Neg. No.	
	Dimensions: – (in cm.)
Acc. 3784	**Collection:** Dr. Ann Fienup-Riordan

103

JEFFREY GIBSON AND THE DIALECTICS OF ADORNMENT

DIETER ROELSTRAETE

One should either be a work of art,
or wear a work of art.

—Oscar Wilde, *Phrases and Philosophies
for the Use of the Young*, 1894

It is one of the lesser, but no less significant, ironies of modernism that one of its primary theorists, the Viennese architect and polemicist Adolf Loos, published his provocatively titled masterpiece *Ornament and Crime* at the tail end of a writing spree that had previously seen him wax lyrical on such seemingly frivolous topics as "Gentlemen's Fashion," "Gentlemen's Hats," and "Underwear." As the austere arch-priest of a pristine, bare-boned functionalism, Loos stands at the source of a powerful, long-dominant undercurrent in modern art history that equates "progress" in art with the purifying drive of the search for some skeletal, unadorned essence or other—an inclination to shed art of all that is deemed superfluous or excessive that reached its theoretical apogee in Clement Greenberg's doctrinaire account of modernist painting in the 1940s, and its most complete practical articulation in the minimalist and conceptual moment of the mid-to-late 1960s, the influence of which continues to be felt across the wide sweep of so-called contemporary art. Indeed, as a practicing architect, as well as an architecture critic, Loos may be regarded as a progenitor of the notion that this cathartic process of purification is best achieved within the confines of the white cube, the blinding light of which was always meant to mercilessly expose all surface effects, in art and architecture alike, as mere rhetorical ruses and redundancies designed to shift attention away from the putative heart of the matter, that of straightforward ("back to basics"), unhampered, and unhindered use. (Already in Loos, one can gain a sense of the mythical white cube's true nature as a *white man's* cube.) Yet Loos invariably made all these assertions while dressed in the immaculate garb of an incurably Anglophile dandy who knew a well-tailored suit when he saw one: a man who at all times appeared deeply invested in, well, *appearances*, "cosmetics." Reductionism, then, yes, but not quite ad absurdum. To conclude these prefatory observations, here are some choice excerpts from *Ornament and Crime*:

> The urge to ornament one's face and everything that lies to hand are the primal origins of visual art. It is the babbling of painting.

> *The evolution of culture comes to the same thing as the removal of ornament from functional objects.*

> This is what constitutes the greatness of our age: that it is not capable of producing a new ornament.

> The modern ornamentalist is a straggler, or a pathological phenomenon.

> We have the art that has supplanted ornament. Once the day's toil and labor is over, we go to Beethoven or *Tristan*. My cobbler cannot do that. I must not take his religion from him, as I have nothing else to put in its place it. But anyone who goes to the Ninth and then sits down to draw a pattern is either a fraud or a degenerate.[1]

Ornament and Crime is a founding document of modernism, yet it is easy to see how, upon its publication in 1908, it immediately inspired both a spirited backlash and a zealous following, and the story of its reception closely mirrors the narrative of modern art history as a dialectical tango pitting the Loosian repudiation of ornament against its aggressive, quasi-militant embrace. (For those readers who are keen, à la Loos, to get to the point: it is of course abundantly clear where Jeffrey Gibson's allegiances might lie in this polemic. His is undoubtedly an art of the *embrace*.) As mentioned before, Loos's ultra-chauvinistic critique of ornamentation—the idea that "lack of ornament is a sign of intellectual power"—constituted the default position of much art theory throughout the twentieth century, much of which did indeed adhere, if only instinctively, to the tiresome dictum that "less is more." Starting in the late 1960s and early 1970s, however—and this is a process that has been accelerated by the increasingly embarrassing association, in more recent years, of the minimalist paradigm with the lifestyle industry, as in the cult of Marie Kondo or the urban legend of Klaus Biesenbach's living quarters, which has made "less" seem more like a *bore*—a defiant counter-critique started to take shape that sought to mobilize ornamentation and practices of adornment as a progressive political force in its own right, and it is no coincidence that the increasingly impassioned defense of these practices and strategies was strongly associated with the rise of the women's and gay liberation movements (the story of the Pattern and Decoration Movement is a convincing art-historical case in point here), and also, to a lesser extent, with the emergence of the American-Indian, Black Power, and Chicano Art Movements: those "others" who were eager to unmask the formerly unquestioned, universalizing aesthetic assumptions of art's Eurocentric mainstream as a parochial tangle of mostly white, mostly male, and mostly heteronormative preoccupations—in other words, those of Adolf Loos and his brethren.[2] One of the defining salvos fired early in this debate was penned by none other than Susan Sontag, who in 1964 published her first major essay in the *Partisan Review* under the title "Notes on Camp" (a quarter century earlier, the same *Partisan Review* had printed Clement Greenberg's landmark "Avant-Garde and Kitsch" essay, a latter-day gloss on Loos's essentialist gospel). Here are some excerpts from Sontag's thinly veiled paean to camp, fully acknowledging that "to talk about camp is to betray it":

> The essence of camp is its love of the unnatural: of artifice and exaggeration.

> Camp sees everything in quotation mark. . . . To perceive Camp in objects and persons is to understand Being-as-Playing-a-Role. It is the farthest extension, in sensibility, of the metaphor of life as theater.

> Camp is the consistently aesthetic experience of the world. It incarnates a victory of "style" over "content," "aesthetic" over "morality," of irony over tragedy.

One is drawn to Camp when one realizes that "sincerity" is not enough. Sincerity can be simple philistinism, intellectual narrowness.

Camp is the answer to the problem: how to be a dandy in the age of mass culture.

Camp taste is, above all, a mode of enjoyment, of appreciation – not judgment. Camp is generous. It wants to enjoy.... Camp taste is a kind of love, love for human nature.[3]

This casual concluding note makes for a magical moment in Sontag's otherwise detached analysis, and recalls what we might refer to as Jeffrey Gibson's own "Notes on Camp," which I have excerpted here from an interview with the artist published in 2018:

Often, kitsch is not viewed as having real consequence. I find people often mean for kitsch to incite campy humor, which leans to the dark side of things while always lightening them up. I wanted to unleash this subversive quality in this body of work.... I also wanted to push kitsch over the top, a strategy found in LGBTQ histories to literally get through difficulty and create community.

True kitsch and camp exist in a space between reality and fiction, turned up and exaggerated. We live in a world that fits that same description, and kitsch and camp are now mainstream marketing and entertainment strategies used for commercial and branding gain. We should be very critical of these uses of kitsch and camp, and the impact they have on our psyches. Heightened and mannered reality and fiction have been conflated. I think we are at a point where truth, transparency, and vulnerability stand out, and that these things can sometimes be read as kitsch and camp within this current context. For me, this place of honesty and transparency shares the most subversive integrity with how we have defined kitsch and camp in the past.[4]

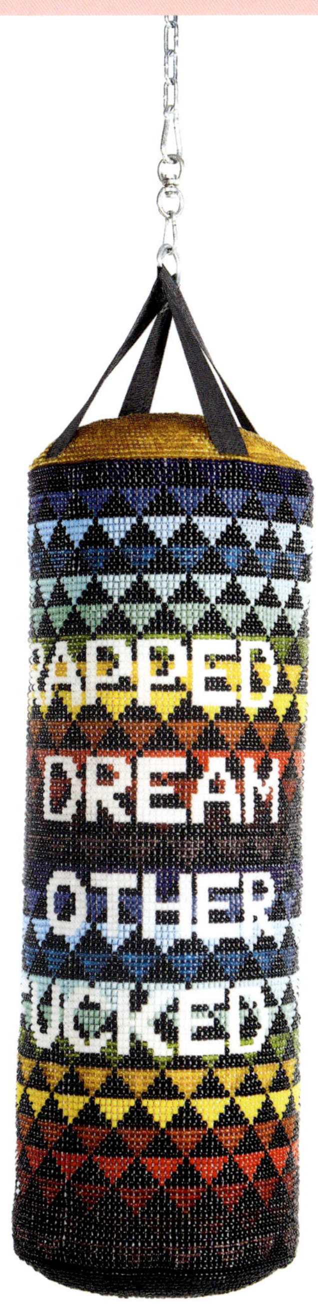

1: Jeffrey Gibson, *TRAPPED IN THE DREAM OF THE OTHER*, 2019. Found canvas punching bag, glass beads, plastic beads, artificial sinew, steel studs, acrylic paint, and steel chain. 67 x 14 x 14 inches (170.2 x 35.6 x 35.6 cm). Courtesy of Jeffrey Gibson and Kavi Gupta, Chicago.

The distinctive shift in tone from Sontag's "Notes," signaling a return to sincerity rather than a further ridiculing of it (because these days, that is what most mainstream politics is "for," which is one of the main forces driving the increasing politicization of camp in contemporary culture), highlights the distance traversed by the notion of camp since the mid-1960s—though the challenge of ornamentation as the sacrament of camp culture remains very much alive in the widespread perception that it is a "problem" that continues to require explaining, a provocation that continues to require defending. The defiance compelled by this enduring bias—the inheritance of Loos and his acolytes—is part of what powers Gibson's politics of adornment as a vigorous rejoinder to the minimalist agenda and its "inclination to shed art of all that is deemed superfluous and/or excessive." To begin with, what is art, other than the most superfluous of all things, and therefore also the most excessive? Isn't this perceived superfluity its very essence, and excess art's sole reason for being—the "proof" of its hard-fought emancipation from the "realm of necessity," and that which distinguishes our culture from "nature"? Indeed, in its knowing celebration of the political implications of such a cultivation of artifice, exaggeration, and excess (and conversely also in its acknowledgment of the invisible political implications of minimalist dogma), Gibson's work discloses something of the indispensable essence of art as anti-essentialist theater, as an apology for "making"—in the literal sense of what an *artifex* does—that complicates the dominant utilitarian worldview of Occam's modernist razor. Something of the militancy of Gibson's take on the politics of ornamentation resonates, I think, in his choice of materials for some of his best-known sculptures, such as *Both Hands* (2014), *ONE BECOMES THE OTHER* (2015), *ALL I EVER WANTED ALL I EVER NEEDED* (2019), and *TRAPPED IN THE DREAM OF THE OTHER* (2019, fig. 1), which, underneath all the appliqué and layers of beading, aren't just punching bags for no reason, and neither are they the only martial motifs in the artist's work, which he himself has likened to a *hammer*.[5] The ornament is worth getting in shape for: we must be ever-vigilant in protecting its blessing from the criminalizing charges of Loos and his ilk.

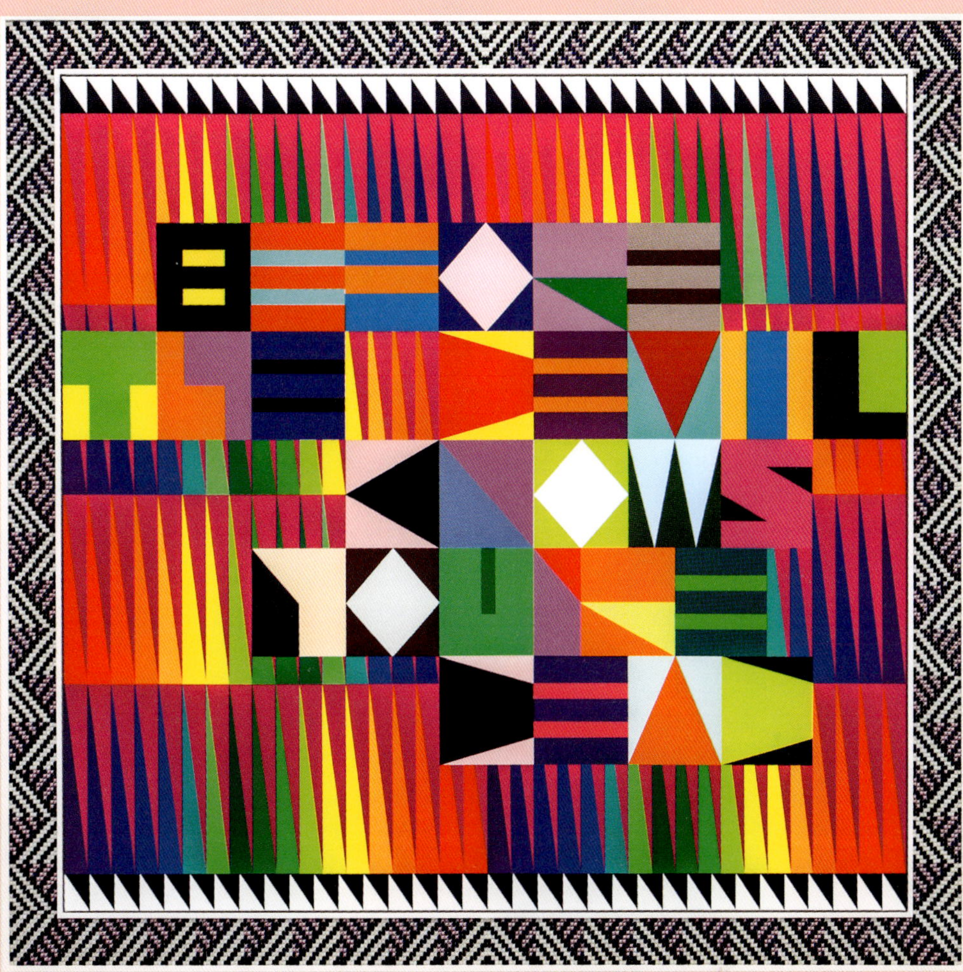

2: Jeffrey Gibson, *BEFORE THE DEVIL KNOWS YOU'RE DEAD*, 2019. Acrylic on canvas, glass beads and artificial sinew inset into custom wood frame. 78 × 78 × 3 inches (198.1 × 198.1 × 7.6 cm). Courtesy of Jeffrey Gibson and Kavi Gupta, Chicago.

It is becoming increasingly difficult, thankfully, to think back to a time when Josef Albers was the only Albers worthy of note in art-historical circles. As recently as 2011, however, one could still hear Liam Gillick declare, in lecture after lecture, "I am more interested in Anni Albers than Josef Albers," followed by the furious scribbles of anxious audiences intent on learning more about the former, and less about the latter. These days, the entire world seems "more interested in Anni Albers than Josef Albers"—more invested, that is, "in the applications of modernism in the lived world as a compromised applied negotiation of contexts than in any notion of purity in relation to the creation of form."[6] It is tempting to view this gradual turning of the tables in terms comparable to those of the ornament's latter-day revenge on the minimalist master narrative of white-cubism: instead of the centralizing thrust of Josef's phallic *Homage to the Square* (1959), we now prefer the disorienting appeal of Anni's radically decentered patterning—echoes of which I cannot help but discern in the angular language and shimmer of Gibson's most recent works (such as *A CHANGE IS GONNA COME* or *BEFORE THE DEVIL KNOWS YOU'RE DEAD* (fig. 2), both 2019, and noting that the activist, bellicose tone of the titles of some of these newer works continues the aforementioned "militant" thrust in Gibson's work). Josef's obsession with squares seems, well, positively square when posited against the immersive lure of Anni's décor, and "application" as a whole seems like a much more viable option in both art and life than the aging insistence on autonomy. (Tangentially, the argument of the epistemological challenge of decentralization and disorientation in particular is one I have been invoking time and again of late to explain the mysterious allure of Pierre Bonnard and Edouard Vuillard's art to myself—nineteenth-century artists whose baroque, psychedelic bourgeois interiors have something quietly, truly revolutionary about them.) But the story of Anni Albers's critical ascent in recent years is also, of course, the questioning and expanding of art-historical canons, which were facilitated so crucially by her exposure to non-Western art traditions, and to pre-Columbian and Meso-American arts and crafts traditions in particular—art worlds that are blissfully and instructively free of both the occidental anxiety surrounding ornamentation and the attendant unease concerning what is "pure" versus what is "applied" in art. Perhaps it is particularly the liberating lilt of the lessons of these "other" art worlds that now resounds most consequentially in Jeffrey Gibson's unapologetic art of adornment.

NOTES

1   Loos's article, which was
    published at the height of
    European colonial power,
    infamously begins with the
    following disturbing simile:
    "The child is amoral. For us,
    so is the Papuan. The Papuan
    slaughters his enemies and
    devours them. He is not
    a criminal. But if modern
    man slaughters and devours
    someone, he is a criminal or a
    degenerate. The Papuan tattoos
    his skin, his boat, his rudder,
    in short everything that lies
    to hand. There are prisons in
    which 80 percent of the inmates
    have tattoos. The tattooed
    people who are not in jail are
    latent criminals or degenerate
    aristocrats." Adolf Loos,
    *Ornament and Crime: Thoughts
    on Design and Materials*, trans.
    Shaun Whiteside (London:
    Penguin Books, 2019), 187–202
    (Loos's italics). This edition
    of Loos's writing contains a
    fifty-page afterword by the
    architectural historian Joseph
    Masheck that seeks to provide
    a critical context for Loos's
    various outrages, starting with
    the caustic premise of his
    screed's titular demonization of
    ornament and ornamentation,
    and the implication that the
    ornamental impulse may mask a
    will to *crime*.

2   Few commentators and critics
    of Loos bother to educate the
    general public on the dark
    side of the wayward paladin
    of minimalism, but it is worth
    mentioning that in the closing
    years of the 1920s Loos was
    tried as a sex offender, having
    molested a trio of working-
    class girls aged eight to eleven
    who had been lured to his
    apartment to pose in the
    nude for a series of painting
    sessions (the architect was
    cleared of the worst of the
    charges). Our familiarity with
    the highly sexualized aesthetics
    of Loos's Vienna (which was
    also Sigmund Freud's Vienna,
    as well as that of Gustav
    Klimt and Egon Schiele)
    notwithstanding, it is hard to
    resist the temptation of reading
    Loos's perverse inclinations as
    a function of the sheer force of
    repression at work behind the
    scenes of both his aesthetic and
    building ethic.

3   Susan Sontag, "Notes
    on Camp," in *Against
    Interpretation* (New York:
    Farrar, Straus and Giroux, 1966).
    I have borrowed the Oscar
    Wilde epigraph to this essay
    from Sontag's text. Note that
    "Against nature!" The battle cry
    of Jean des Esseintes, the effete
    and reclusive protagonist of
    Joris-Karl Huysmans's fin-de-
    siecle classic *Against Nature* (*À
    Rebours*, 1884), looms large in
    Sontag's sexual theory of camp:
    "Camp taste draws on a mostly
    unacknowledged truth of taste:
    the most refined form of sexual
    attractiveness (as well as the
    most refined form of sexual
    pleasure) consists in going
    against the grain of one's sex."
    Elsewhere, Sontag speculates,
    in an attempt to "explain the
    peculiar relation between Camp
    taste and homosexuality" (it
    is worth noting here that the
    publication of "Notes on Camp"
    predates the Stonewall riots
    by about half a decade), that
    "homosexuals have pinned

their integration into society on promoting the aesthetic sense"—and that camp, in this view, is their "solvent of morality."

4   Tracy L. Adler, "Introduction and Interview with Jeffrey Gibson," in *Jeffrey Gibson: This is the Day* (New York: Del Monico / Prestel, 2018), 29–30. The body of work referred to here are the "garments" produced in the period 2017–18, some examples of which are titled *Without You I'm Nothing*, *Watchtower*, *A Wag A Wit A Witness*, and *A Little Bit Louder*.

5   *Jeffrey Gibson: Like A Hammer* (Denver: Denver Art Museum, 2018).

6   Bartholomew Ryan, "9 Artists: Bartholomew Ryan on Liam Gillick," Walker Art Museum, June 24, 2014, https://walkerart. org/magazine/9-artists- bartholomew-ryan-on-liam- gillick.

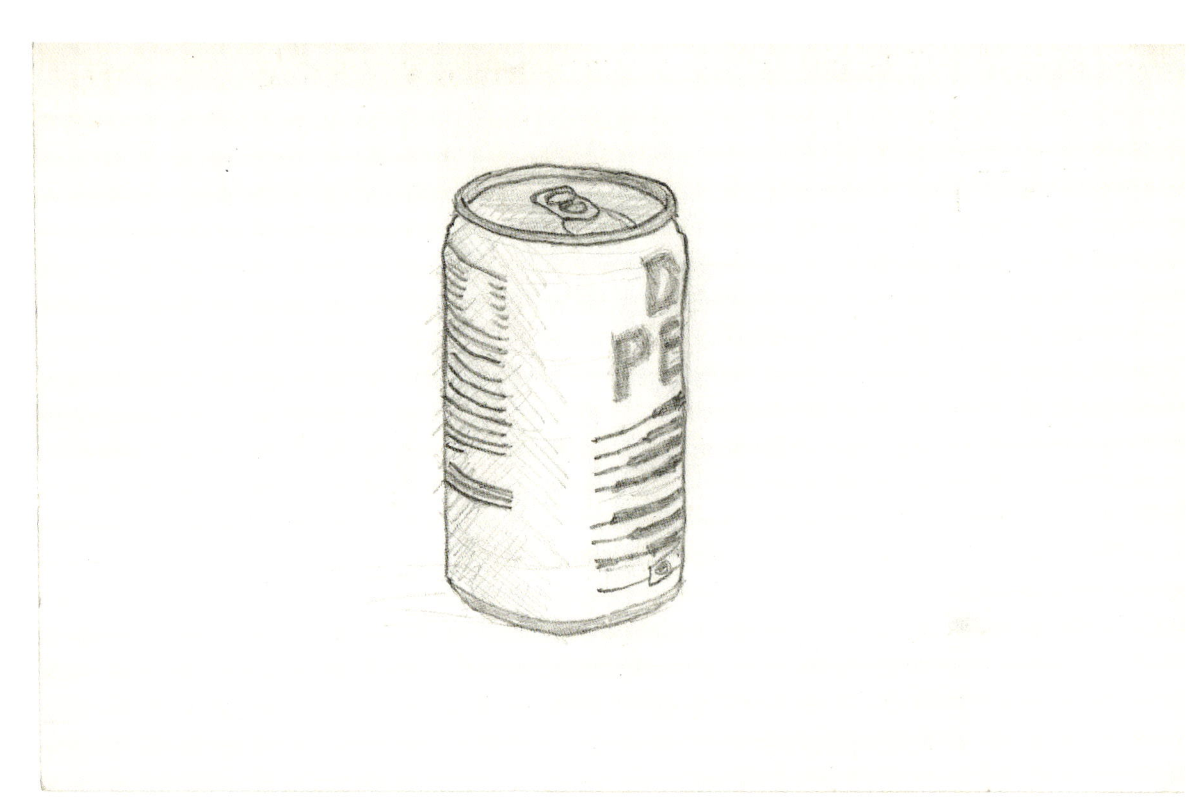

Provenience: Toksook Bay, Nelson Is., Alaska

People or Culture: Yupik Eskimo

Object: soda pop

Material: —

Description: "Diet Pepsi" (1 can - 12 oz.)

Used as gift in seal party.

Dimensions:
(in cm.)   —

Collection: Dr. Ann Fienup-Riordan

ON THE MAP

KATHLEEN ASH-MILBY

It was a winter day in 2002. As the curator at American Indian Community House Gallery in New York City, I was working my way through a stack of mail, including a nice fat envelope of slides from an artist I did not know named Jeffrey Gibson. This bevy of imagery intrigued me; the bright organic abstraction was not the type of unsolicited work I typically received from artists looking for opportunities to exhibit their work. This was something very different. I needed to know more and contacted Gibson immediately to set up a studio visit. I had no idea at the time that two decades later, for collectors and museums across the United States, Jeffrey Gibson would be one of the most sought-after Native artists, if not one of the most prized contemporary artists, working today.

At the time, Gibson was working in a shared studio space in Brooklyn. He explained that these paintings were an extension of a series of abstract works he titled *Infinite Anomaly*. To me they appeared as primordial landscapes that could have read as underwater, alien, or even microscopic environments, they were so hyperreal. Vivid neon colors and amorphous shapes oozed across and lifted off the surfaces, sometimes dripping over the edges, as in *The First Principle* (2004, fig. 1). It was pure joy in form and texture that teased the mind and delighted the senses. As we looked at some of these paintings together and talked about his recent work, he spoke about feeling the need to wash away all the baggage that came with being a Native American artist and a desire to create a new imagined environment, as if from scratch.

Many people who are now enjoying his work have no previous experience with Native art and are approaching it without sufficient context for understanding its deep cultural and historical complexity. The work of being a Native American artist extends beyond engaging in the creative process to include the weight of cultural responsibility within the lived experience of being Native American. As people, as parents, as future ancestors, we often end up in the position of educators, whether we like it or not. As an Indigenous curator of Native art for more than twenty-five years, I also carry the responsibility of moving the field forward by educating peers and supporting artists like Gibson, who transcend artificial boundaries and challenge

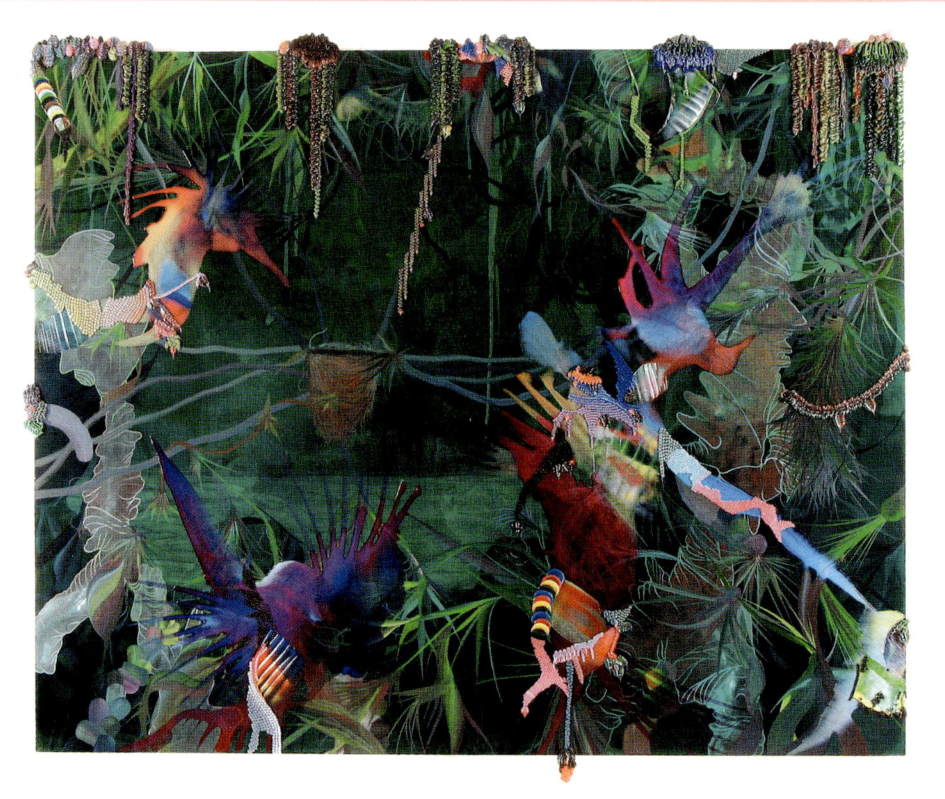

1: Jeffrey Gibson, *The First Principle, 2004.* Oil and silicone on panel.
47 x 55 1/2 inches (119.4 x 141 cm). Courtesy of Jeffrey Gibson.

expectations. At the time, I think both of us shared frustration that the art world barely registered Native art.

Within these paintings he created an imaginary world that existed before people, full of possibility, but without the weight of history. "The burden of identifying as Indigenous in a western culture to me was laden with trauma and grief and despair," he reflected recently.[1] It wasn't that he was denying the reality of those histories, which had impacted his family: "But when I think about my grandmothers and I think about everything they've accomplished in their lifetimes, it was not about despair and grief, if anything it was about ingenuity, it was about faith, it was about perseverance, it was about family. . . . it's about having to negotiate a really difficult set of challenges." For many Native people, it is a very specific type of poverty that our families have experienced and continue to experience, which he described as, "this never-ending thread" that connects so many disadvantages: commodity food, tribal housing, poor healthcare and education, high mortality rates, boarding schools. "It's not just about surviving. At what point can you put some of this burden down long enough to take a breath and think a new thought, write a new sentence, imagine a new future?"

Gibson and I have very different backgrounds in many ways, although we both grew up comfortably middle-class, spared the hardships of our parents' and grandparents' generations. His father, James Gibson, was a civil employee of the US Army, and a member of the Mississippi Band of the Choctaw; his mother, Georgia, is a citizen of the Cherokee Nation. Gibson and his sister grew up like many so-called army brats who lived a semi-itinerant childhood hopping across the globe from air force base to air force base. They understood their cultural connections and identity as rooted in family and personal histories in Oklahoma but were also fully immersed and engaged in a middle-class, cosmopolitan lifestyle that included living in Germany, South Korea, and later, for Gibson, attending graduate school in London. His childhood was privileged in ways his grandparents could never have imagined.

I immediately understood his reasons for wanting to break free and could see that his work was a radical affront to stilted expectations. I, too, was frustrated by the art world; its categorical boxes limited and confined our art and expression, if it was considered at all as art, rather than cultural artifact. It was as if critics and contemporary art curators had hysterical blindness; it was right there in front of them, but they refused to see it. I knew immediately that I wanted to help Jeffrey Gibson's work be seen and understood. Yes, it was Native American art, but it was also unabashed in its embrace of the many influences on his practice: the 1980s alternative music and club scene, the swirling graffiti splattered around his neighborhood, the explosive colors and movement of Plains dance regalia, and the effusive decadence of Haudenosaunee stacked beadwork.[2] And it was quite plainly about desire—an emotion and identity that was rarely expected or accepted in the field of Native art.

"I probably would have felt comfortable talking about [this work] in terms of desire," he said, but they were also inspired by the work of less well-known nineteenth-century American painter Martin Johnson Heade (1819–1904), who created lush, romanticized tropical landscapes full of what he perceived as exotic flora and fauna (fig. 2). Heade's paintings present a fertile and uninhibited natural environment that must have seemed antithetical to the buttoned-up, prudish urban culture of the Victorian-influenced society he occupied. The intensity of color was in stark contrast to the dark, stultifying environment of the East Coast cities where Heade lived during the early Industrial Revolution. It is hard not to read them as expressing some sort of pent-up desire for the sensual.

Although Gibson's paintings from 2004 to 2005 can be interpreted through an erotic lens, he describes them as about the "carnal, desirous side of looking at something you find beautiful." Artists who expressed an Indigenous and queer identity through their work were rare at the time. It isn't that queer, Indigenous artists were hiding their identities, but there was little art that openly and plainly celebrated gay love and desire.[3] After Gibson's solo exhibition *Indigenous Anomaly* in 2005 at the American Indian Community House Gallery, and his inclusion in the group exhibition *Off the Map: Landscape in the Native Imagination* in 2007 at the National Museum of the American Indian, both in New York, his daring, sensual paintings and sculptural work began to attract critical attention.

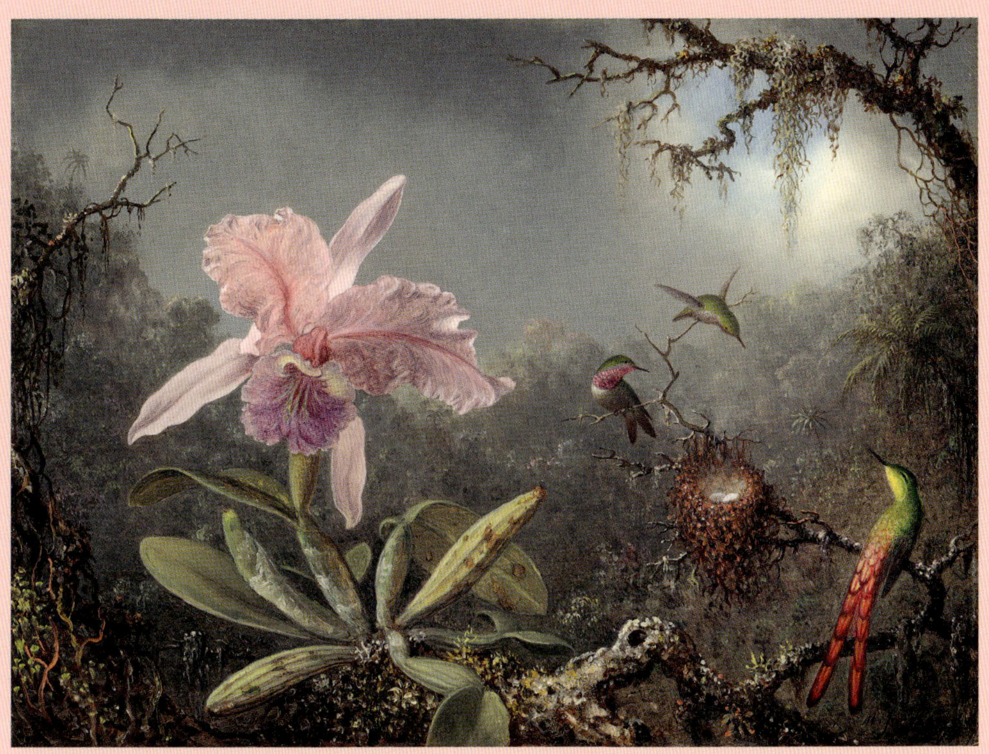

2: Martin Johnson Heade, *Cattleya Orchid and Three Brazilian Hummingbirds*, 1871. Oil on panel. 13 11/16 x 17 15/16 inches (34.8 × 45.6 cm). Courtesy of the National Gallery of Art, Washington, DC.

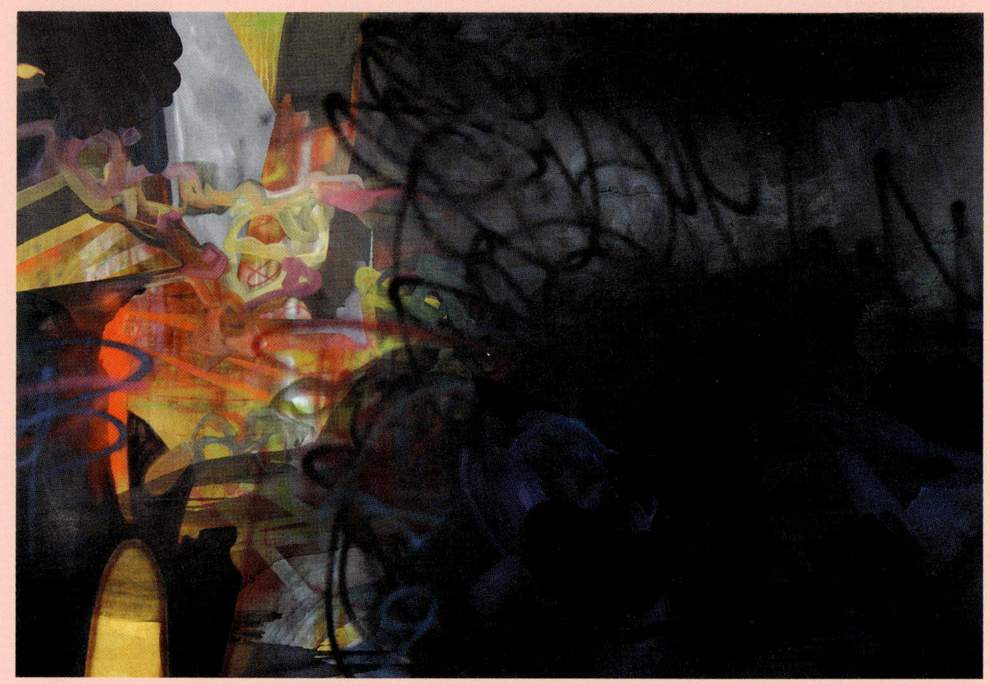

3: Jeffrey Gibson, *Submerge*, 2007. Oil and spray paint on canvas.
    84 x 120 inches (213.4 x 304.8 cm). Courtesy of Jeffrey Gibson.

Despite the success of this exuberant work, an unspoken darkness had already begun to edge in. The energetic color in *Submerge* (2007, fig. 3) seems to be in the process of being aggressively tagged by black graffiti and submerged in darkness. His semi-sculptural works from this time look charred, as if some environmental poison or apocalyptic event has descended upon his imaginary world. Gibson created these works after a visit with his grandmother and her property in Oklahoma, which came into the family through a government land allotment in 1906 under the Dawes Act of 1887.[4] He wanted to explore the idea of memory embodied in the land and soon learned about the complicated, intimate entanglements of family history and painful, personal trauma associated with this place. "I started thinking of the land as a witness to all of this and tried to personify this in my work."

He soon broke away entirely from the organic dimensional work—including his use of pigmented silicone and foam—that was quickly becoming his hallmark. Gibson has described this as a time of reckoning; while beginning to achieve recognition in the Native art field he was also beginning to question the direction of his work altogether and his decision to be an artist. The immediate association of his work with silicone by non-Native viewers as emulating beadwork was particularly irksome. While he was admittedly inspired by the decadence and dimensionality of turn-of-the-twentieth-century Haudensaunee stacked beadwork, he was not trying to re-create beadwork in his art. He saw this equivalency as a superficial interpretation based on his ethnicity; these audiences were searching for easy points of reference rather than allowing for the recognition of his work as emerging from his experiences as a full person. "It was the beginning of me really thinking about the difference between showing something to a primarily white audience versus an Indigenous audience and people of color."

At one point in frustration he destroyed previous work, washed the canvases, and repurposed the material, creating vivid but visually unhinged riots of pattern, color, and imagery (*Quixotic*, 2009, fig. 4). This unresolved and uncomfortable work represented a dramatic period of flux for Gibson as he struggled to find new mooring for his work and to understand what was missing, to find his own voice. "I

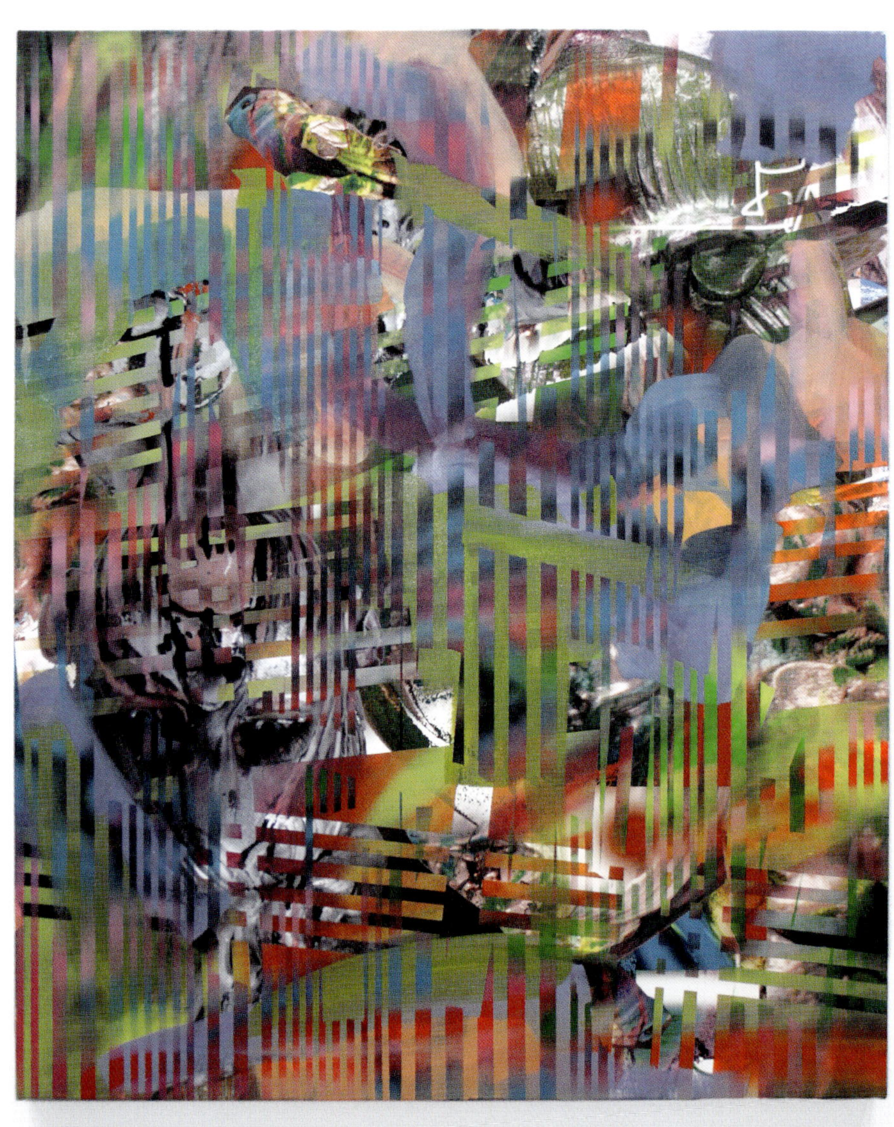

4: Jeffrey Gibson, *Quixotic*, 2009. Oil and spray paint on
    printed canvas. 40 x 32 inches (101.6 x 81.3 cm). Courtesy
    of Jeffrey Gibson.

think when you come from a family like mine that worked very hard to acculturate and to be middle-class American, you are trying to find that voice that was not just about fitting in and blending in." In high school and college, he had no peers who understood the context of his work. "There was no conversation to be had, no one understood where I was coming from." Instead, he wrestled with these ideas through his art, and in front of an audience, searching for this voice.

Eventually the weight of history and trauma must be confronted. For Gibson this necessity meant facing his identity as a Native American artist and all it entails—the good, the bad, and the ugly. He spent time with other Native artists and practitioners who worked with long-standing Native forms, materials, and aesthetic conventions, including beadwork. He began working with hide, melding his enduring love of graphic abstraction with an irregular, organic surface, as in *Constellation No. 7* (2012, fig. 5). By 2013, his experimentation with format had led to his incorporation of beads, jingles, and fringe mass-produced for the contemporary powwow market. He reinterpreted these materials, applying his fascination with color and geometric abstraction and engaging with popular culture through text. His punching bag series was an especially piquant expression of this new direction, in its aesthetic transformation of a powerful symbol of machismo into queer beauty, as well as through the unsettling, implied reference to violence against Native women. In using what could be referred to as Native craft items made specifically for the tourist trade, the sculptural work included in this exhibition raises even more complicated questions about the consumption and reuse of Native American materials.

Much of Gibson's recent work embodies a shift away from trying to help a non-Native audience understand the Native experience, to speaking directly to an expanded audience who identify as Indigenous, people of color, or LGBTQ+. This work has often engaged directly with community members, inviting them to be a part of a performance or experience. In *To Name An Other* (2019), for example, fifty people from these diverse backgrounds performed together, reciting messages of resilience, power, and pride with fearless affirmation. These words were also emblazoned on brightly hued garments and hand drums designed by Gibson.

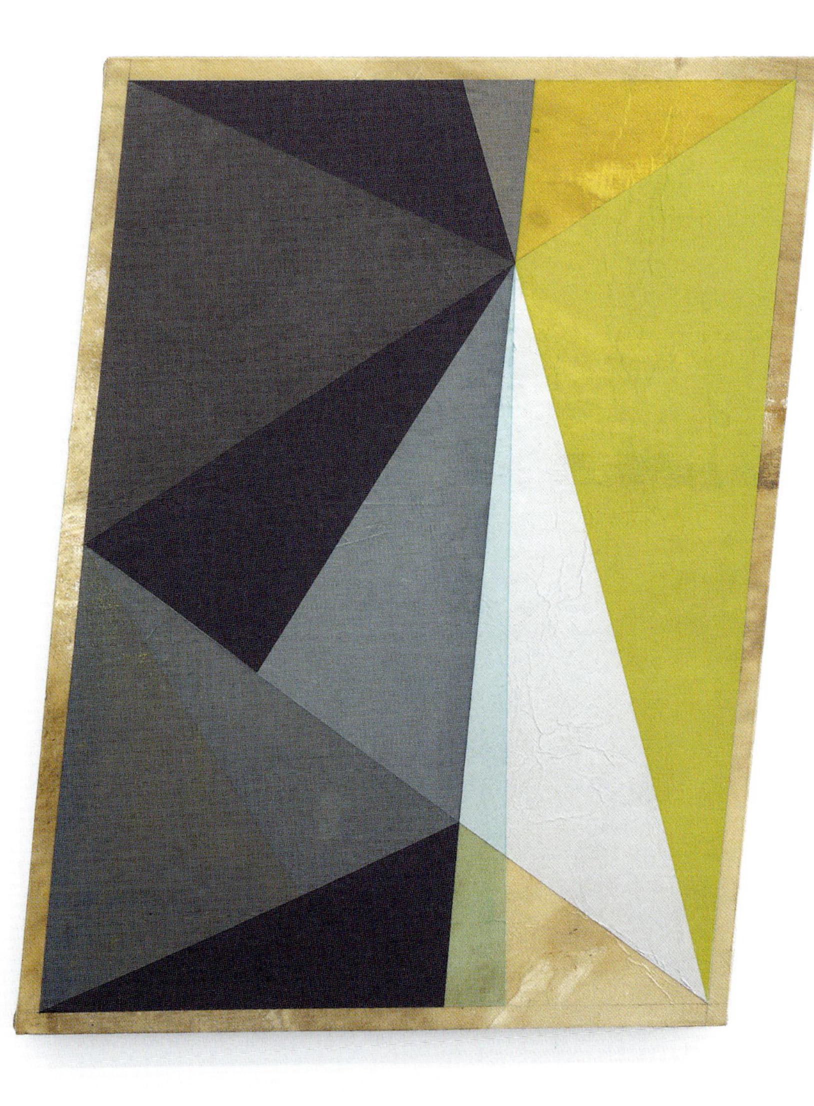

5: Jeffrey Gibson, *Constellation No. 7*, 2012. Acrylic on deer hide–covered wood panel. 22 x 18 inches (55.9 x 45.7 cm). Courtesy of Jeffrey Gibson.

She Never Dances Alone (2020, fig. 6) a multiscreen installation reached an even broader audience when it was shown in New York City's Times Square. His largest scale new media work to date, it spanned sixty screens. This invigorating, visually stunning work focuses on a dancer, Sarah Ortegon, performing a jingle dress dance across multiple screens accompanied by an excerpt of music by A Tribe Called Red.[5] The jingle dress and the dance associated with it are a symbol of healing that has become an intertribal expression of female empowerment.[6] Although the video begins with Ortegon looking down across the audience and then up to the sky, her dancing figure soon multiplies and fragments into a dizzying kaleidoscopic of frenetic geometric shapes and colors, becoming a celebration of color and light.

Twenty years after that first studio visit and conversation, Gibson has found some reconciliation with the weight of responsibility and trauma we carry as Native people. By using his art as a vehicle for supporting one another and creating spaces for healing, he continues a deep Native tradition. The art of remixing and innovating with new materials is both the essence of Native art and evidence of cultural resilience, but so is recognizing your accountability to your ancestors and your community. After years of fighting for recognition, Native art and Jeffrey Gibson's art are finally and firmly on the map of the art world, but his most important audience lies elsewhere. Ultimately his art embodies values passed on to him from his grandmothers: it is about heart, ingenuity, faith, perseverance, and family.

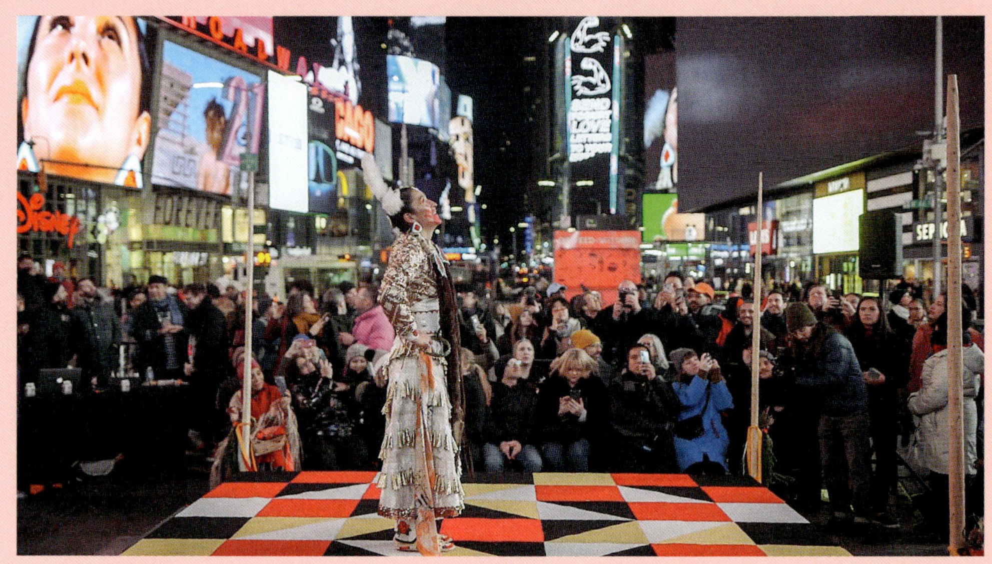

6: Jeffrey Gibson, *She Never Dances Alone*, performance still.
Times Square, New York City, March 7, 2020.

NOTES

1   All quotes from Jeffrey Gibson, personal communication with the author, Zoom interview, December 31, 2021.

2   Haudenosaunee (or Iroquois) stacked or raised beadwork is characterized by the layering of beads to create a sculptural or three-dimensional appearance.

3   Kent Monkman, an artist with a very different approach to the subject, who is now well known for his expansive oeuvre of romantic, sensual, and overtly homoerotic paintings using the trope of early Western nineteenth-century historical painting traditions, was also meeting resistance to his work as he sought an audience beyond Indigenous art spaces in Canada during this same time.

4   The Dawes Act (1887) was a US law passed to divide communal tribal lands into individually owned land allotments for the purposes of converting the property to individual ownership, and ostensibly to pressure Native people into a farming economy.

5   A Tribe Called Red is known today as The Halluci Nation. The excerpt is from their song "Sisters," ft. Northern Voice, from *Nation II Nation*, 2013.

6   Oral history accounts trace the jingle dance and attire to Ojibwe communities around the time of the 1918 influenza pandemic (1918–20).

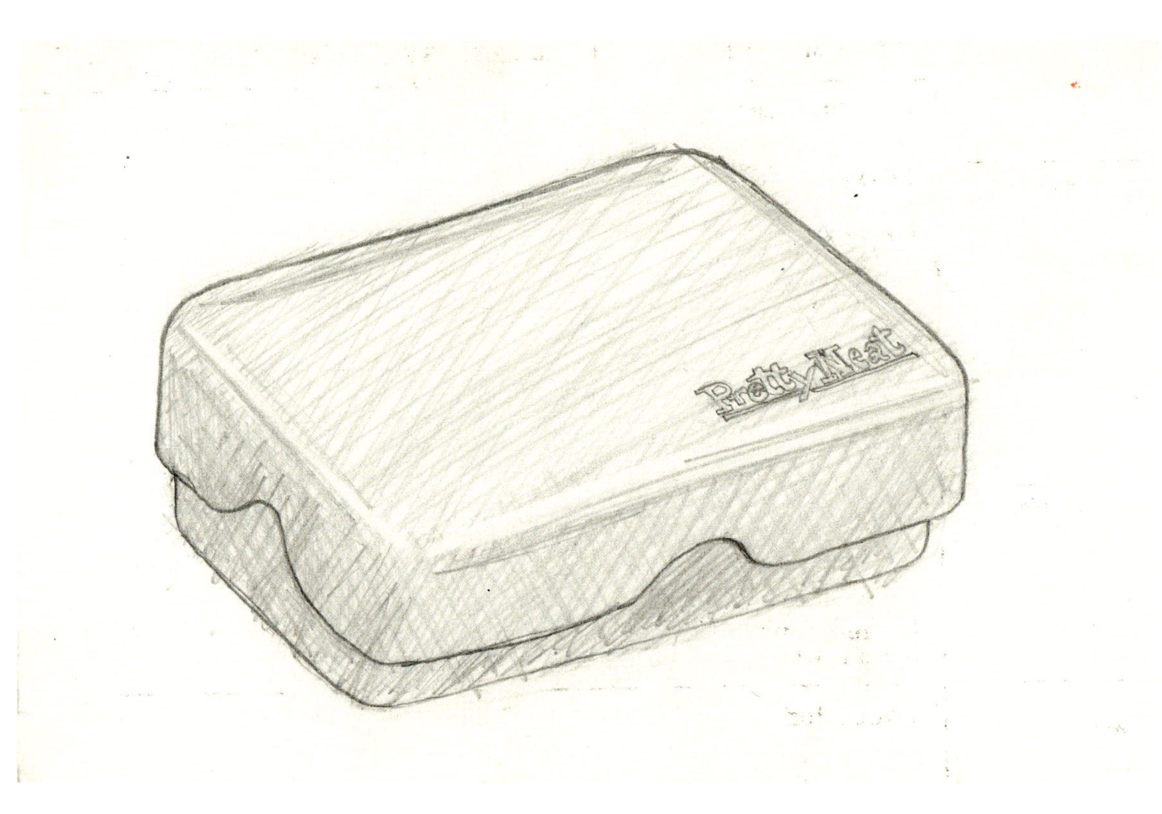
Pretty Neat

FIELD MUSEUM OF NATURAL HISTORY—ETHNOLOGY 2-2

Provenience: Toksook Bay, Nelson Is., Alaska

People or Culture: Yupik Eskimo

Object: soap dish

Material: plastic

Description: "Pretty Neat", red.

Used as gift in seal party.

Dimensions: 11.0 cm l. x 8.5 cm w. x 4.5 cm h.
(in cm.)

Collection: Dr. Ann Fienup-Riordan

133

PLATES:
GIBSON

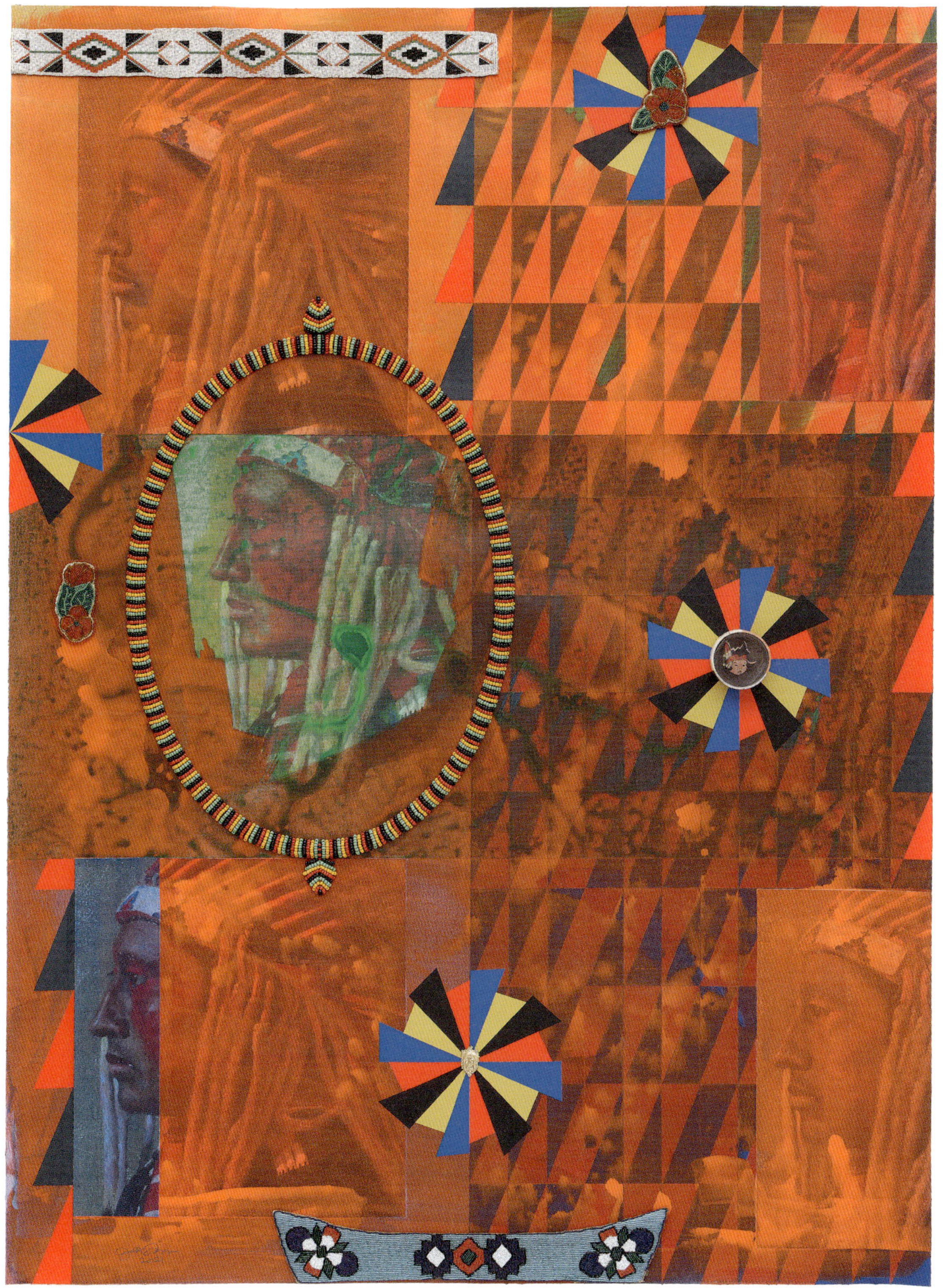

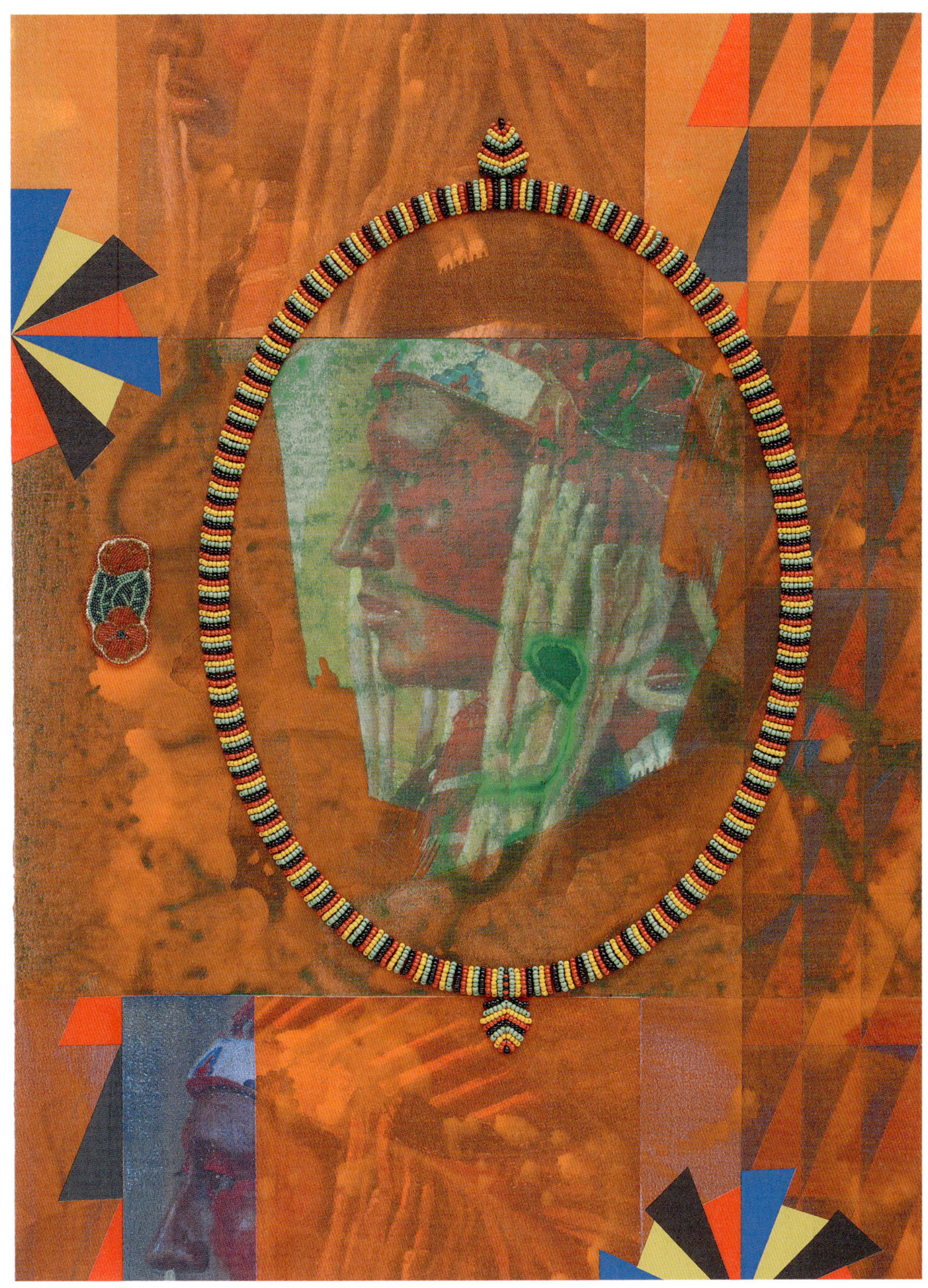

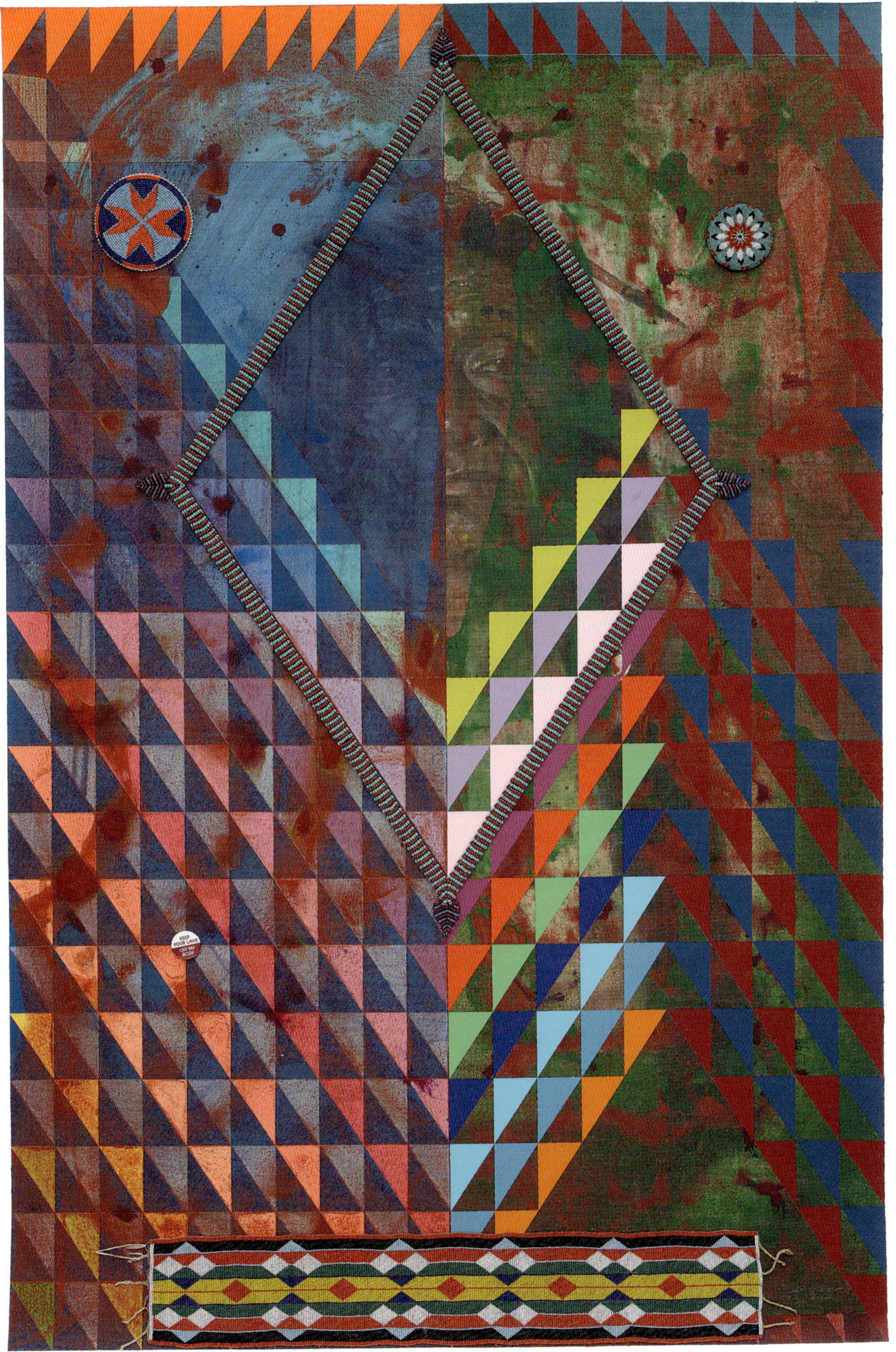

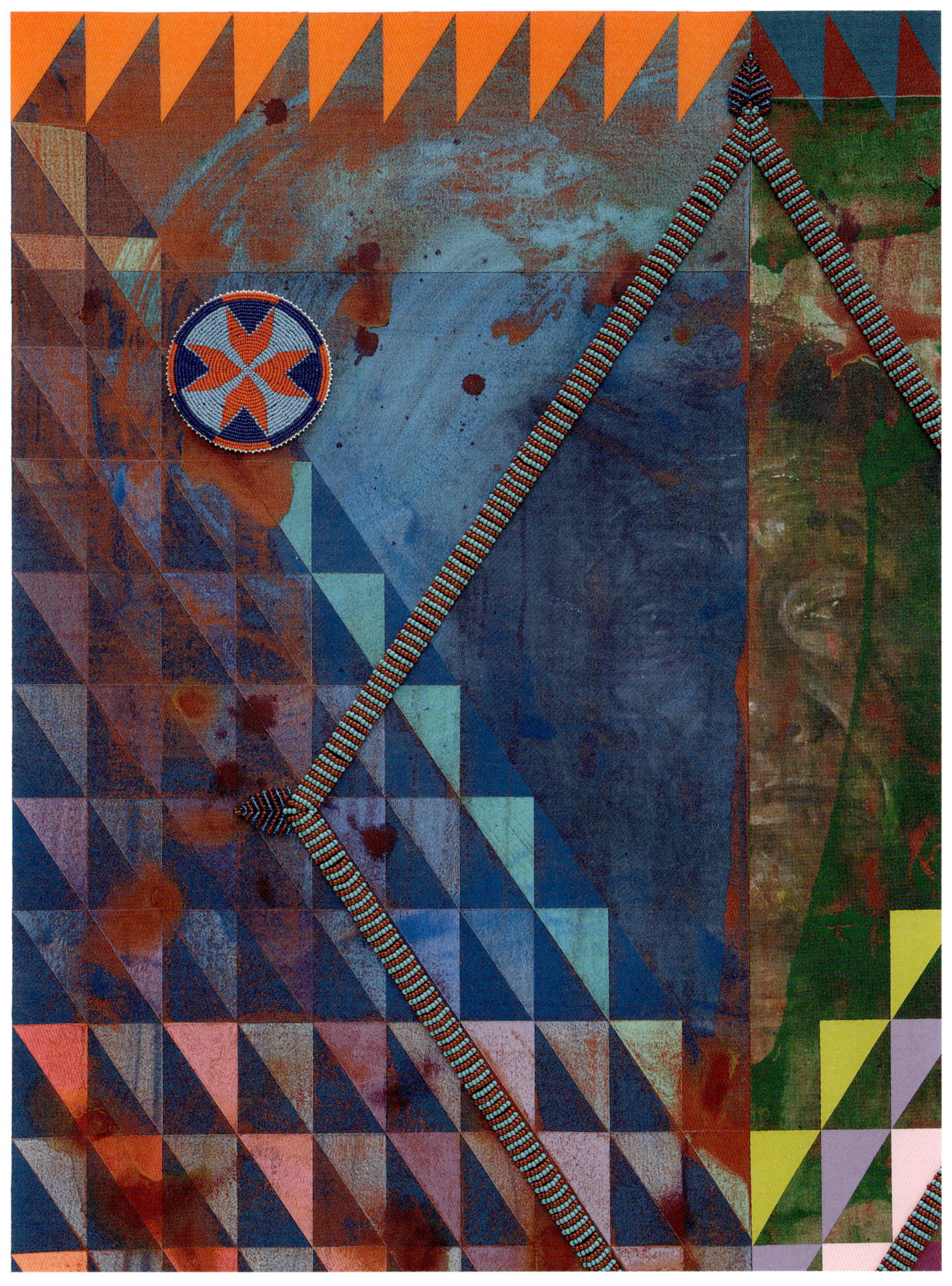

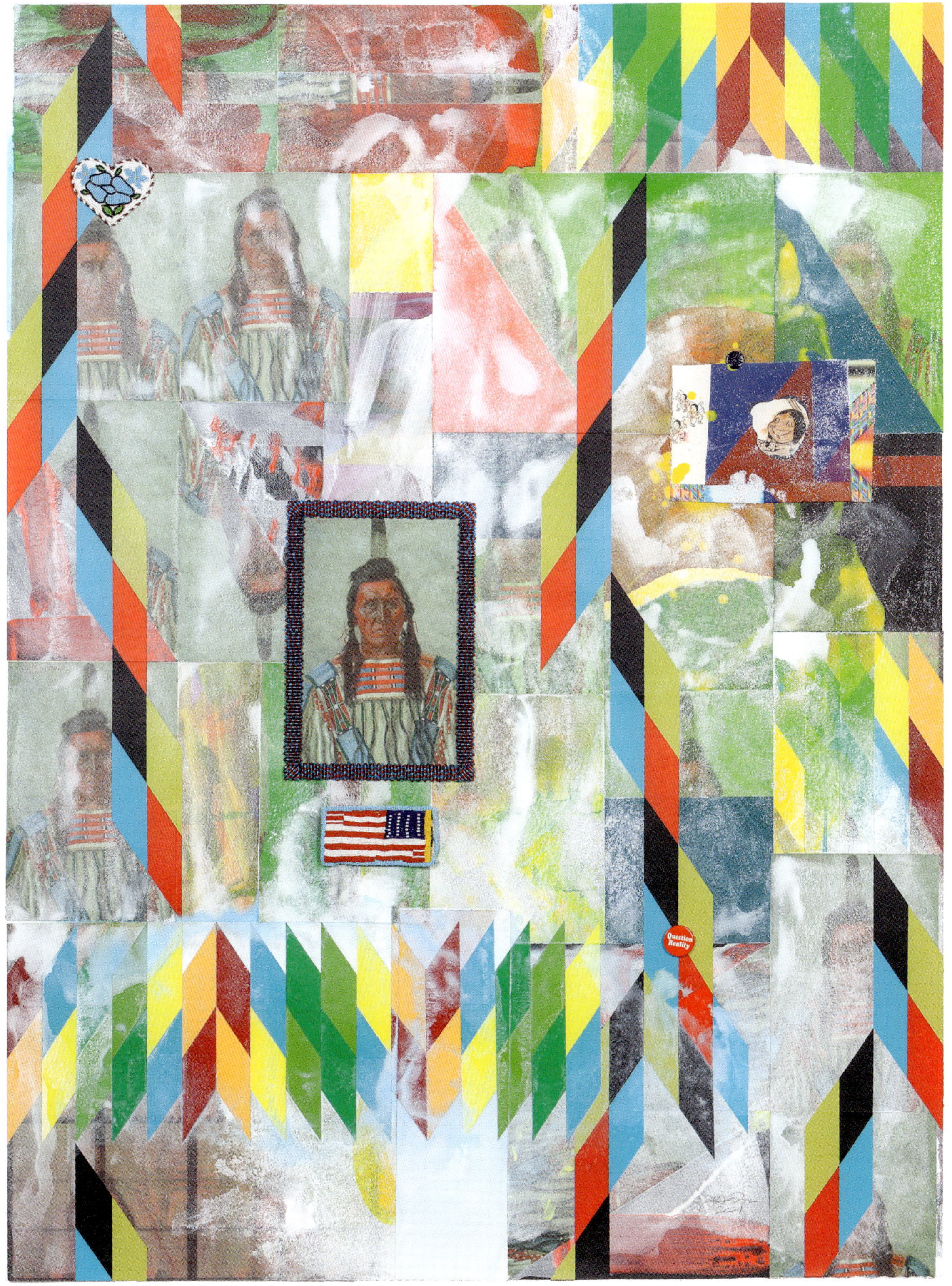

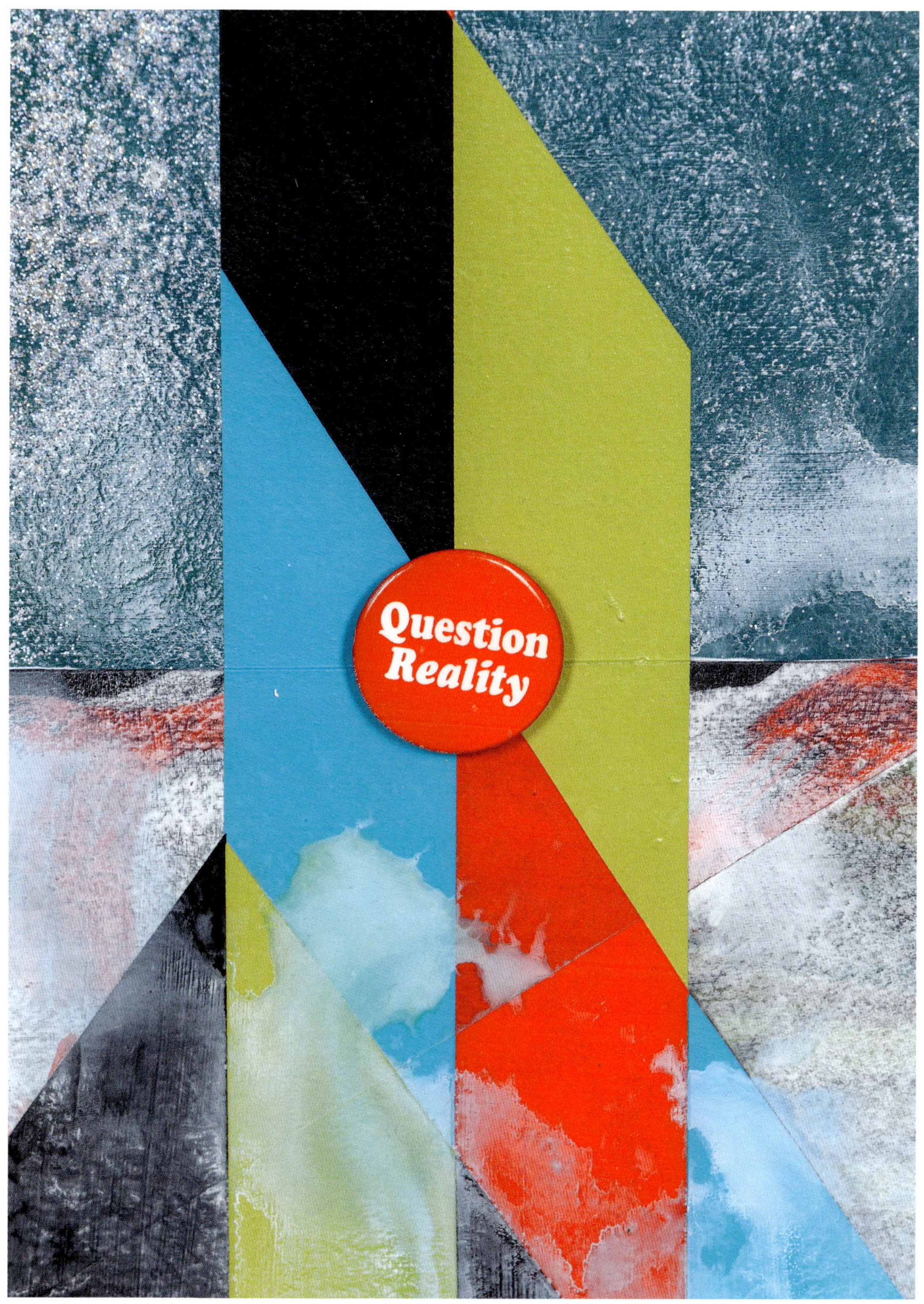

Question
Reality

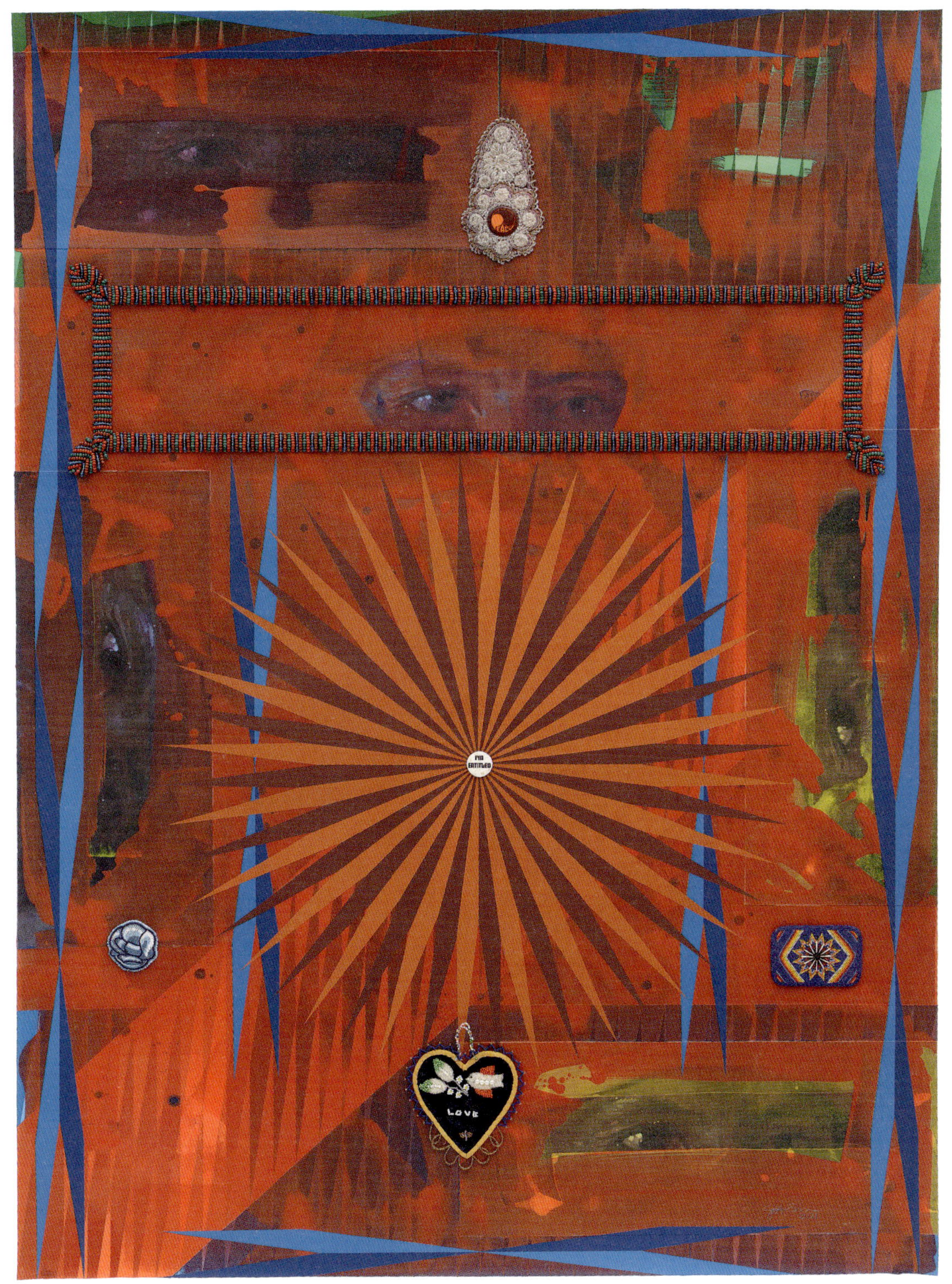

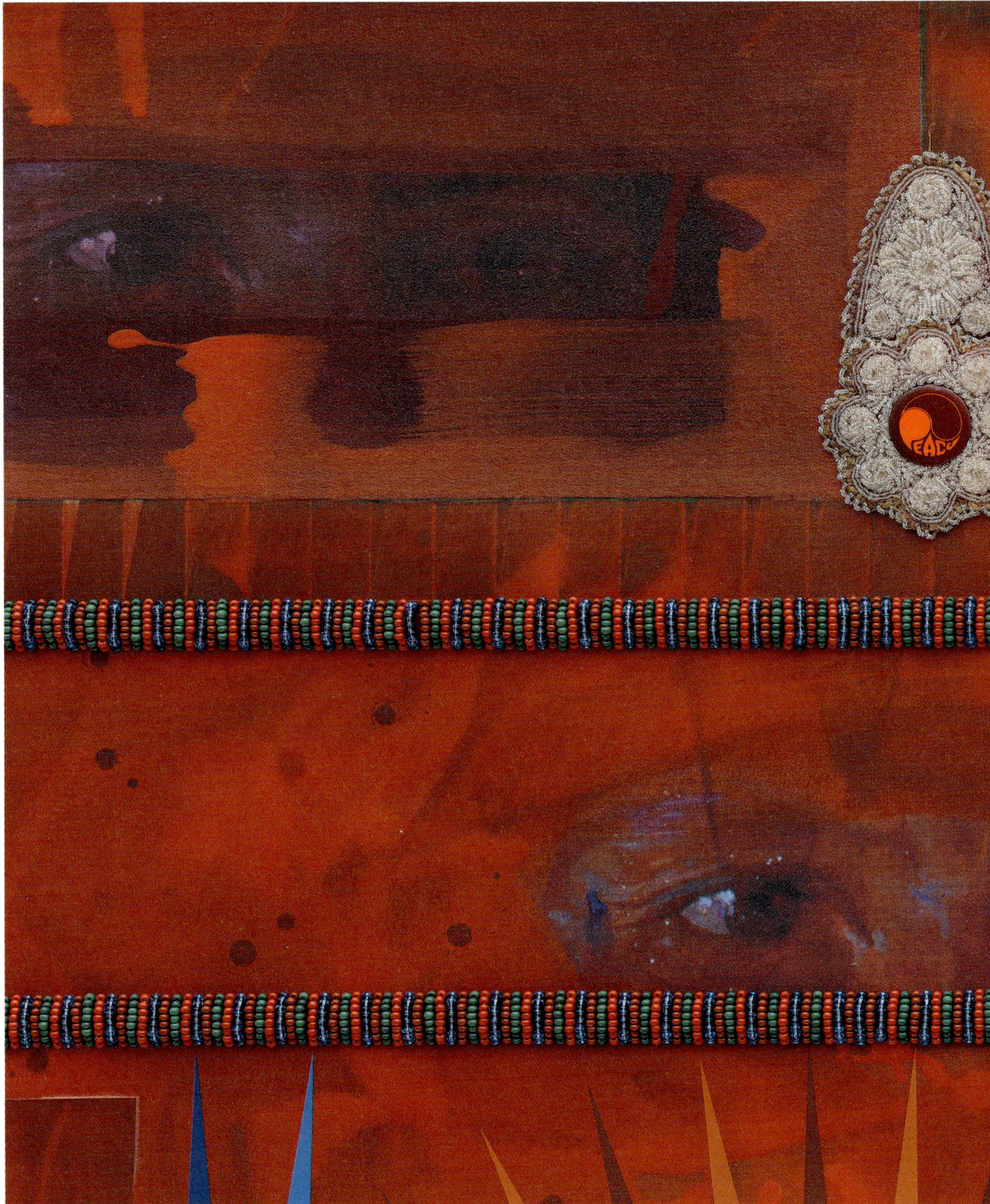

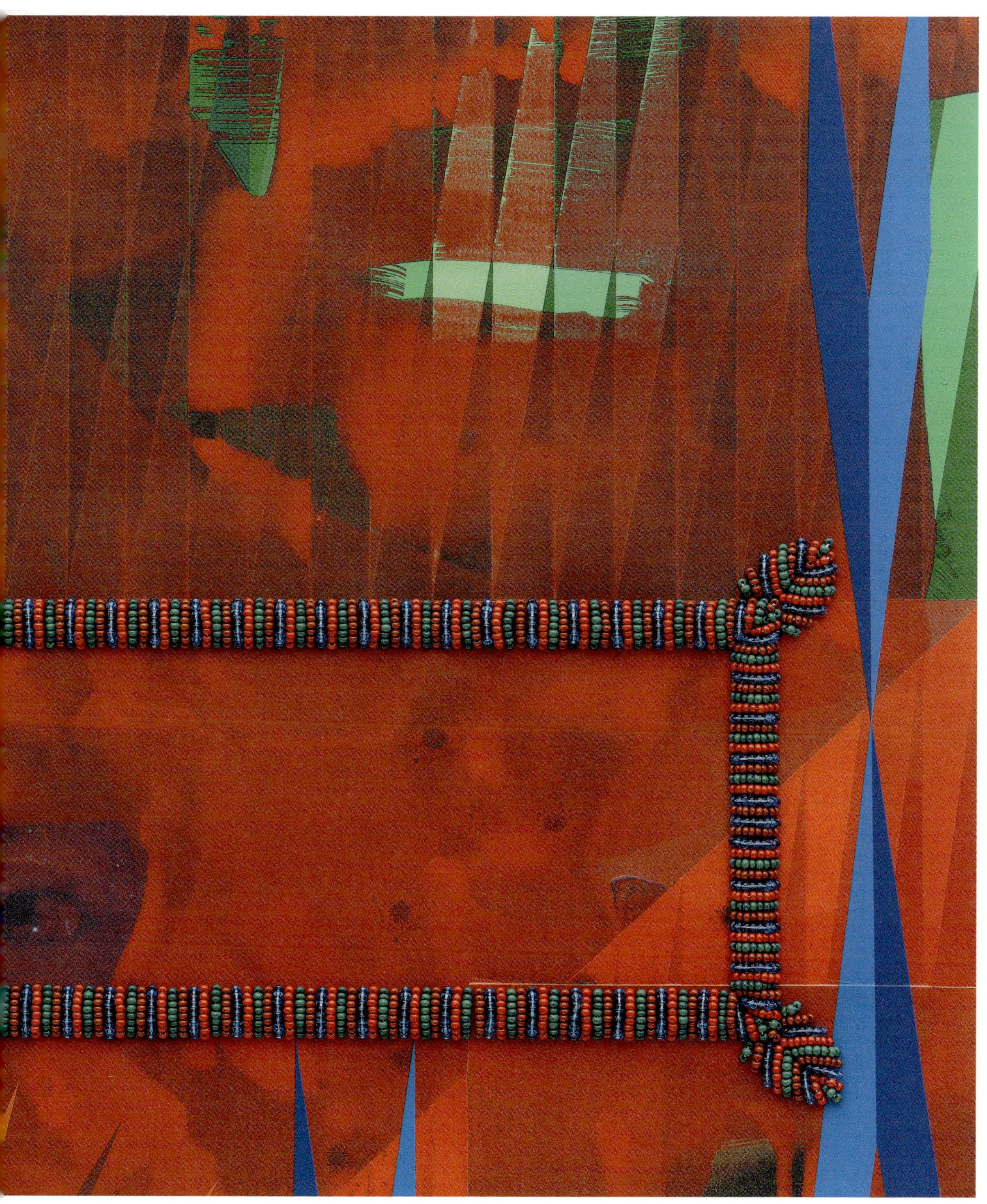

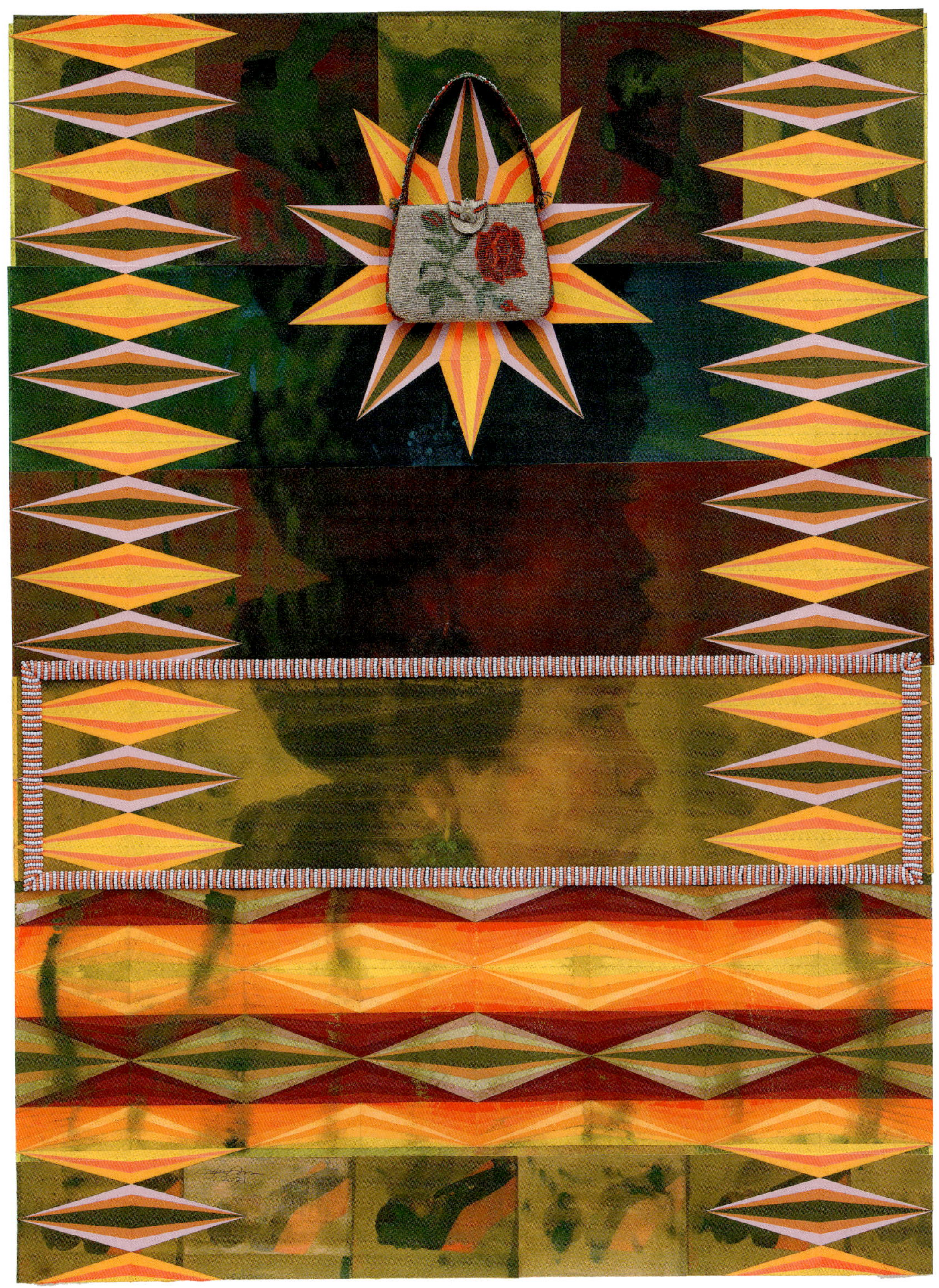

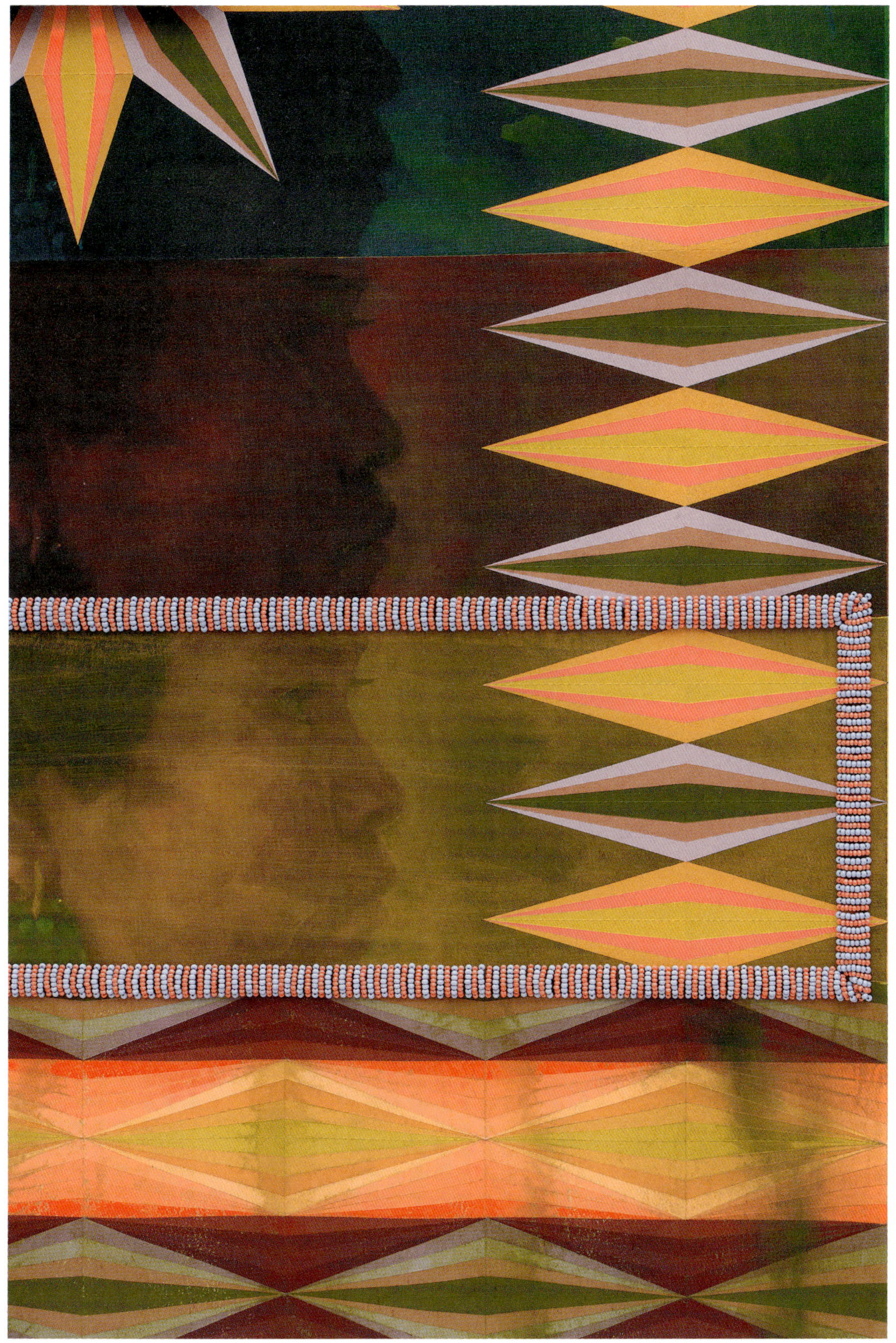

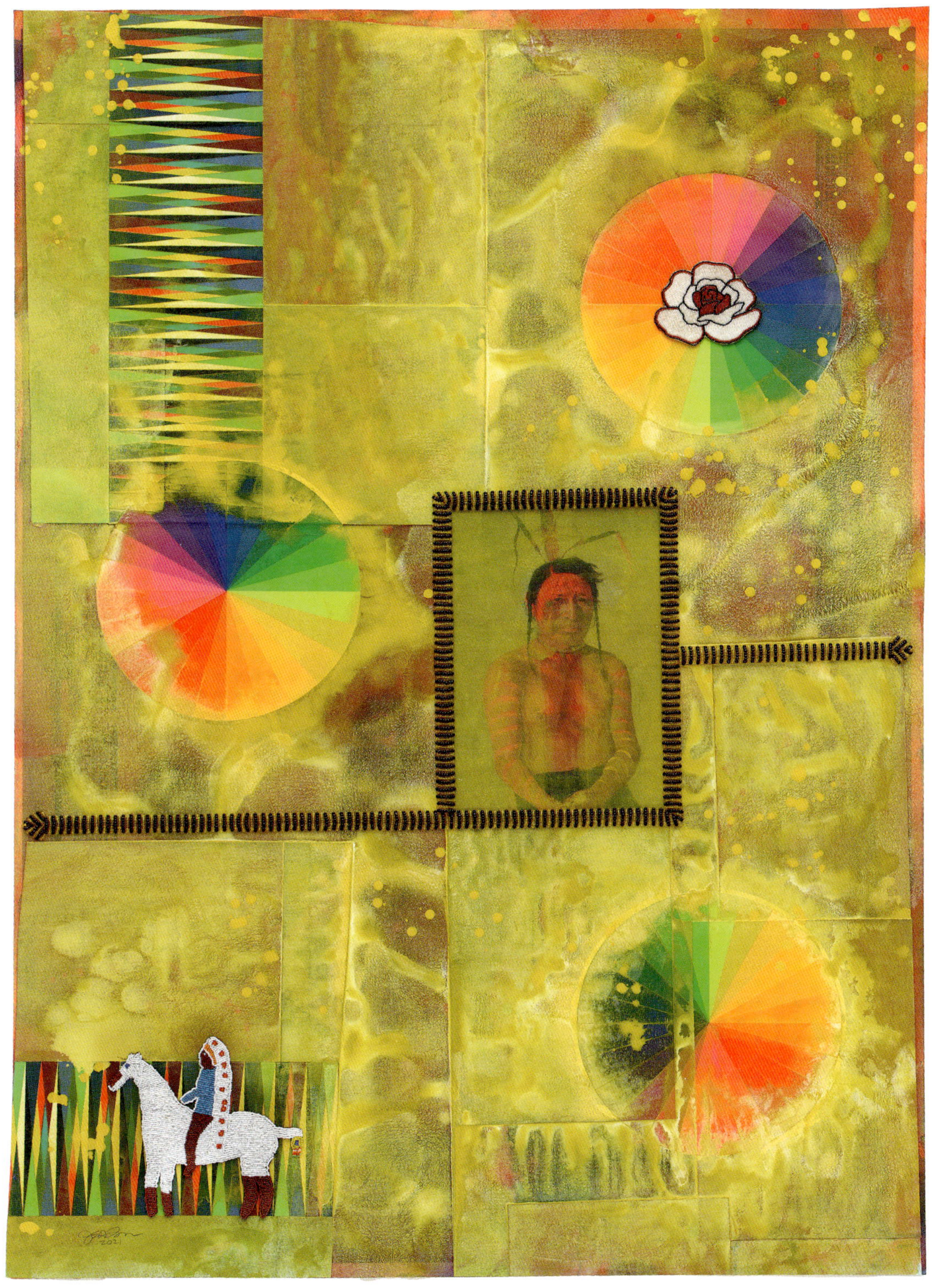

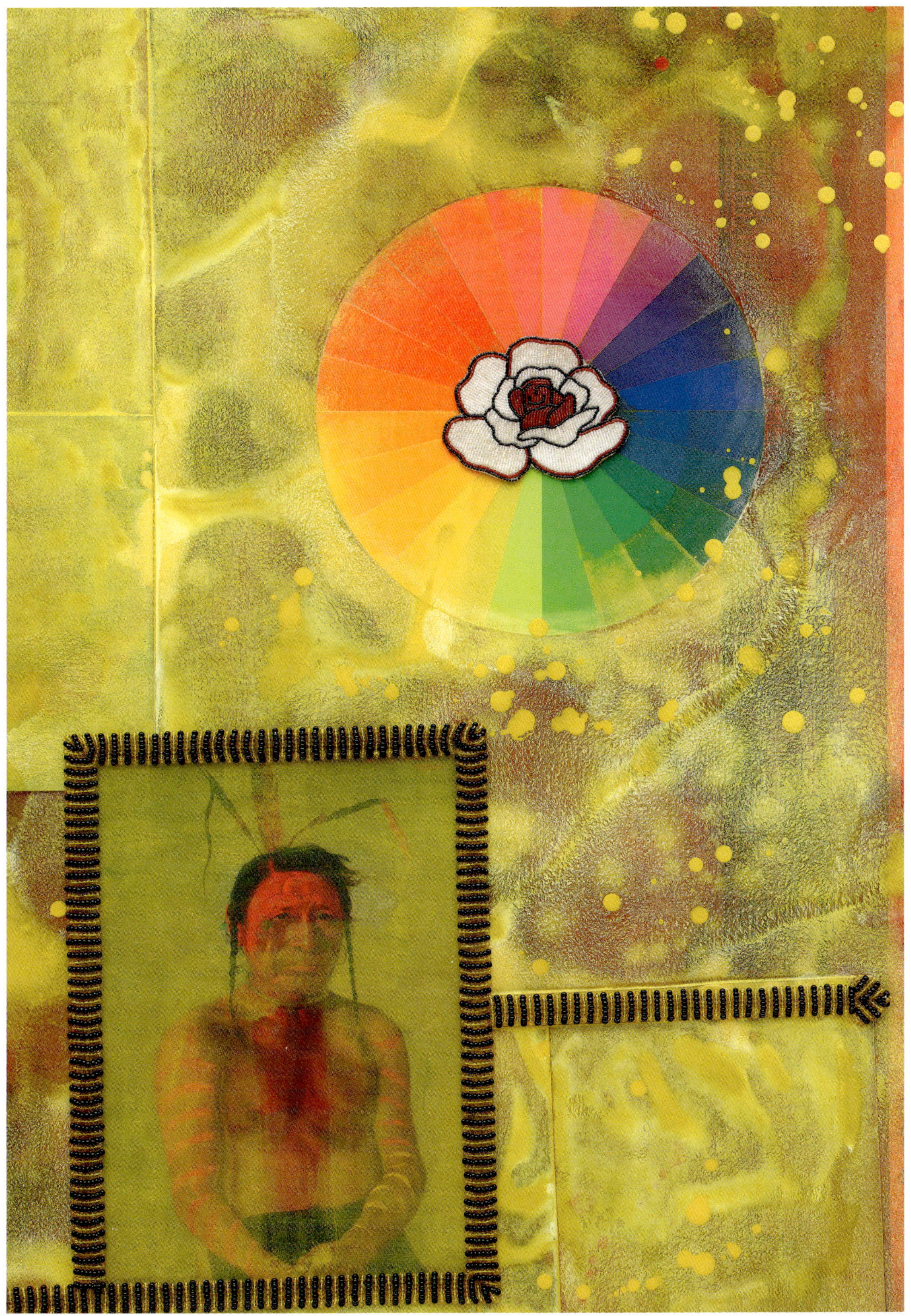

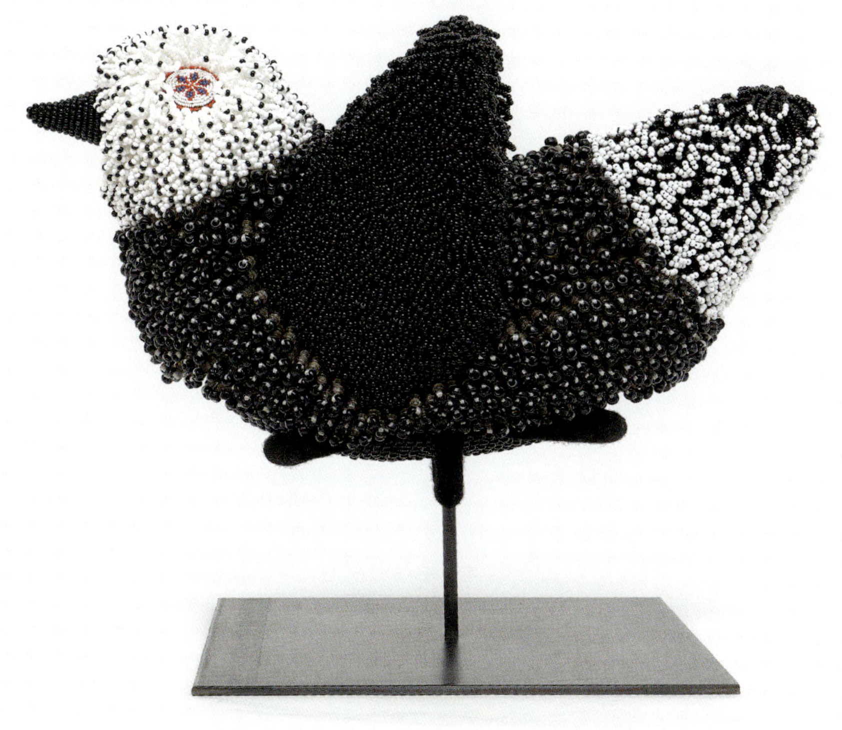

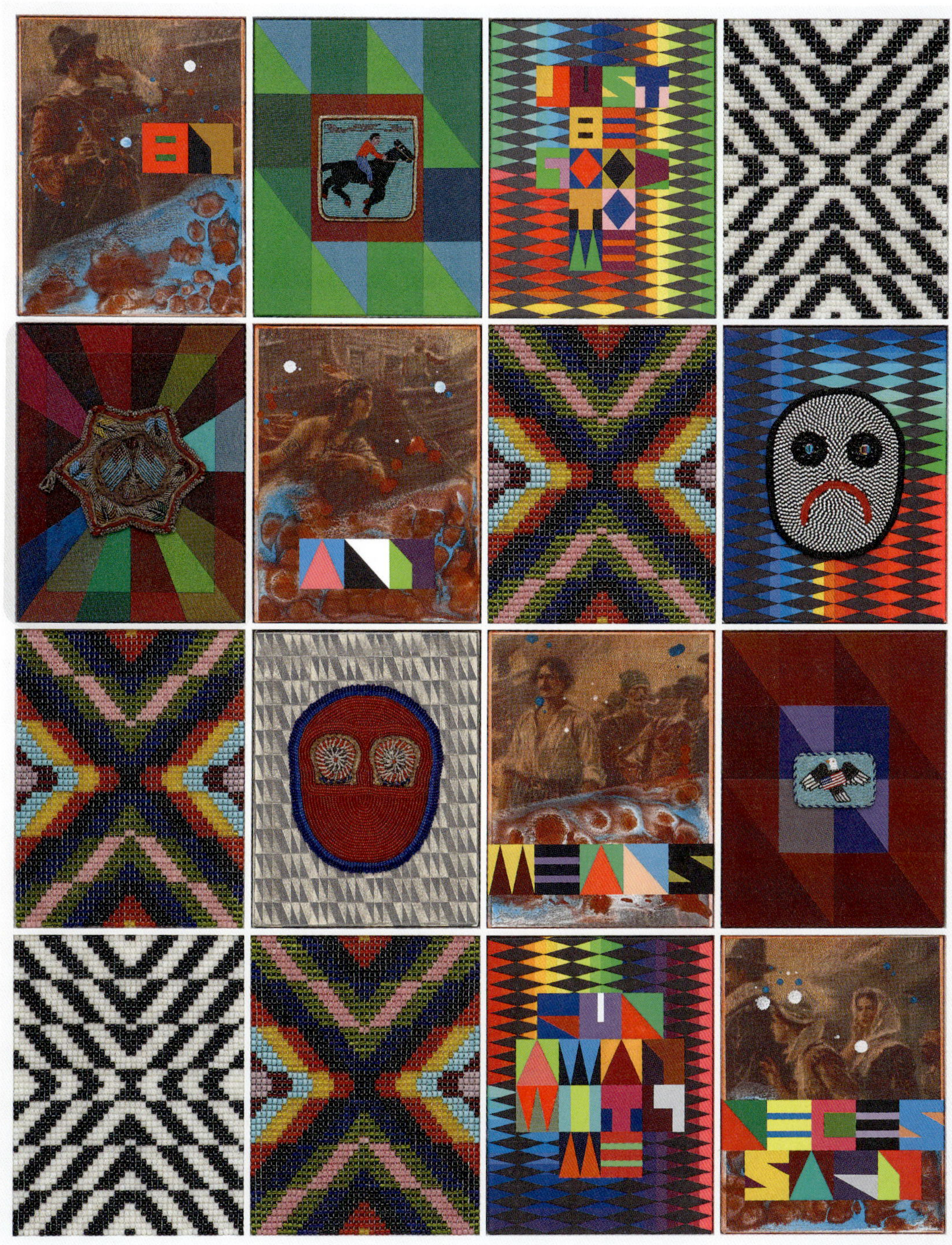

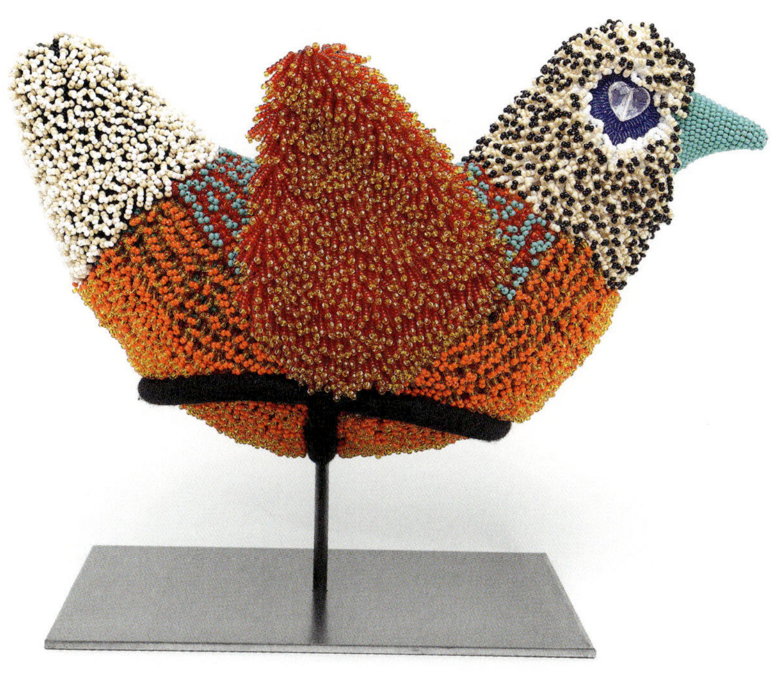

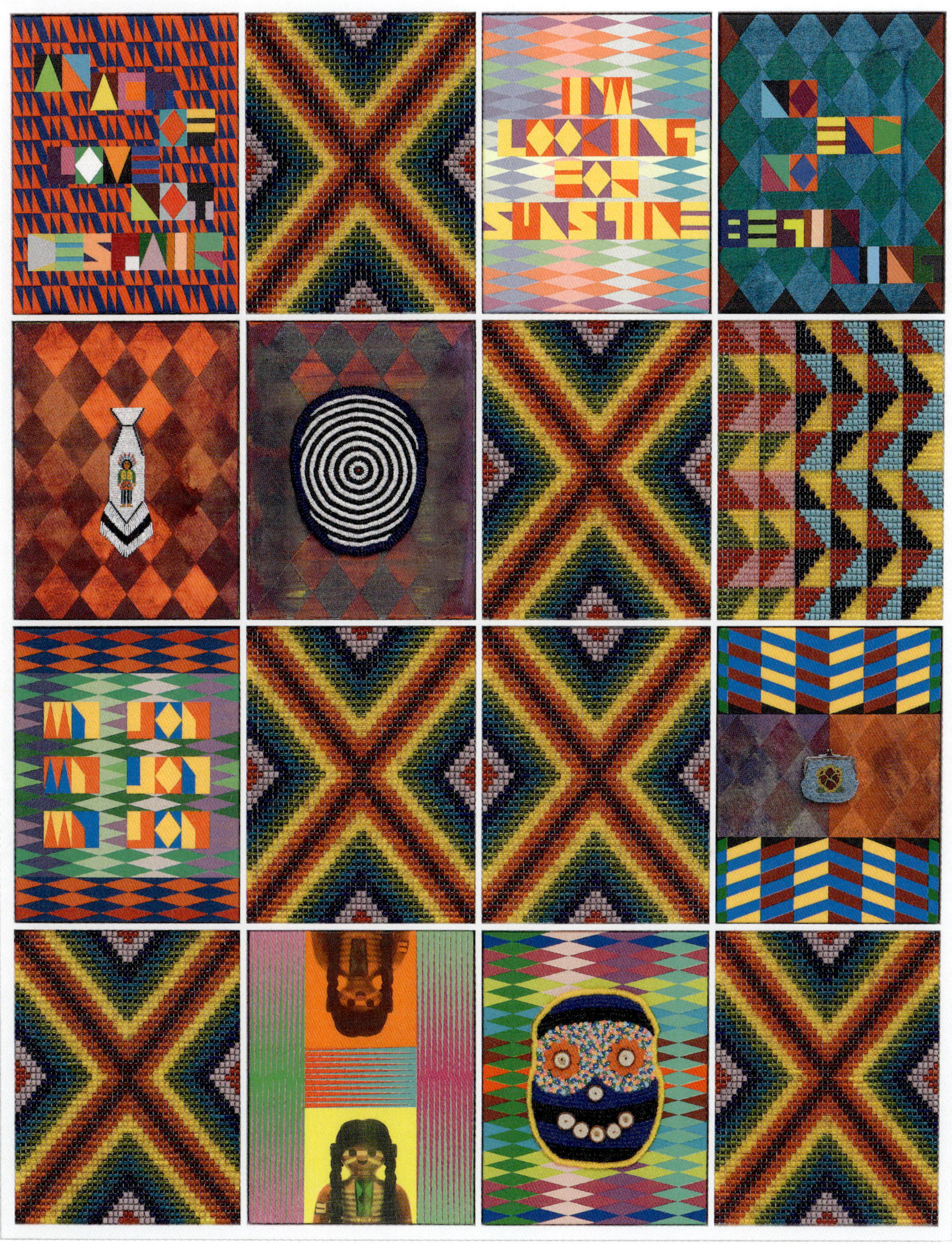

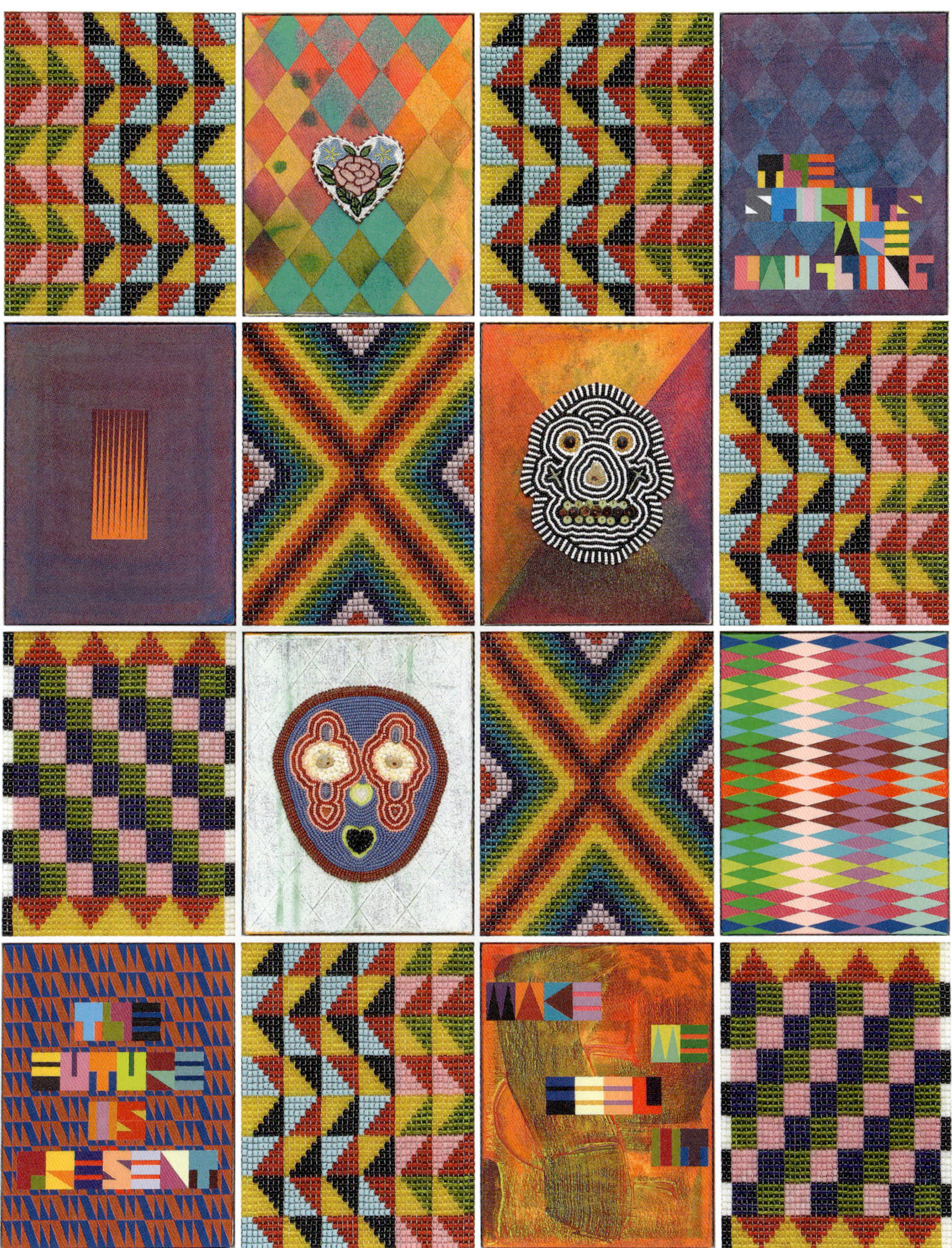

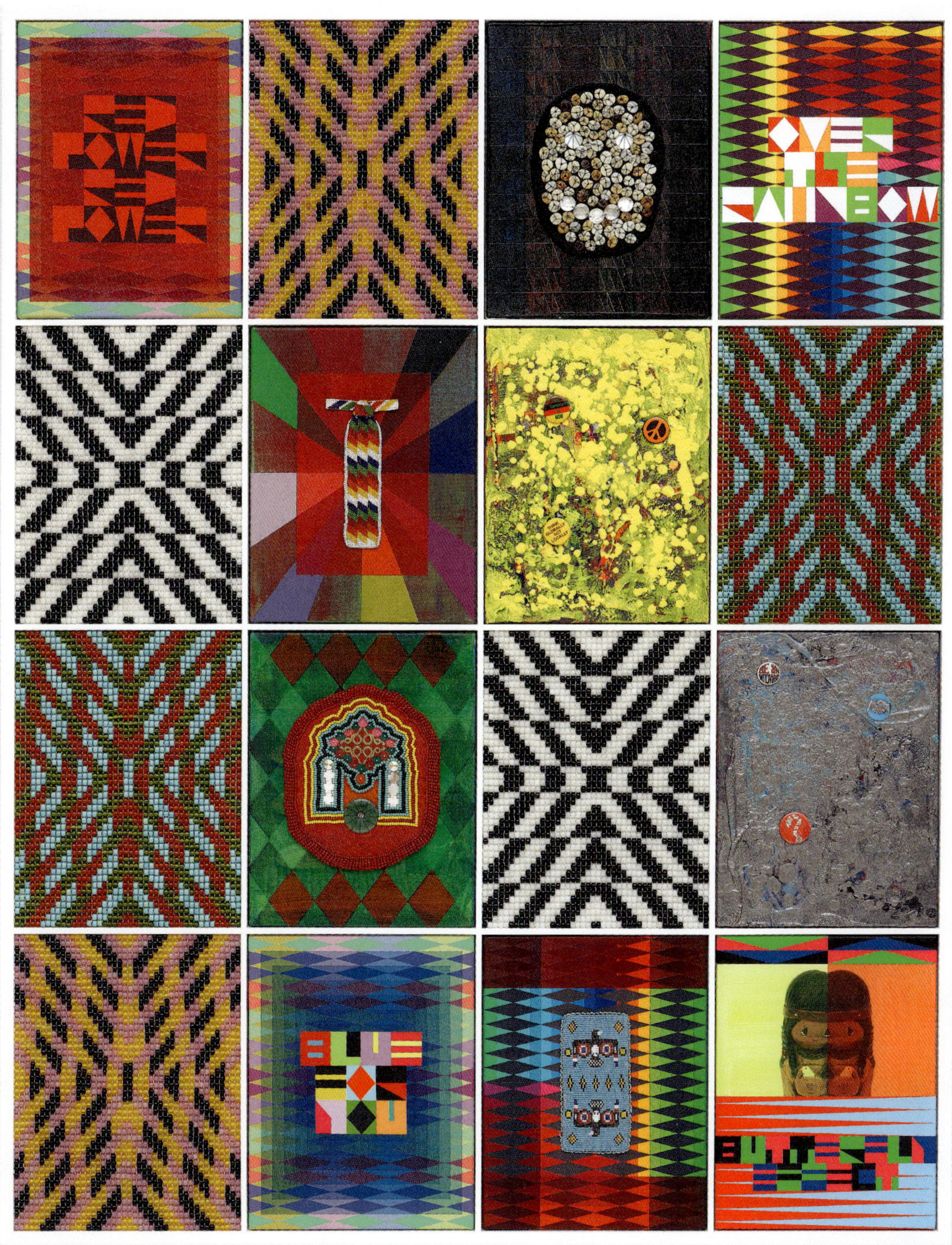

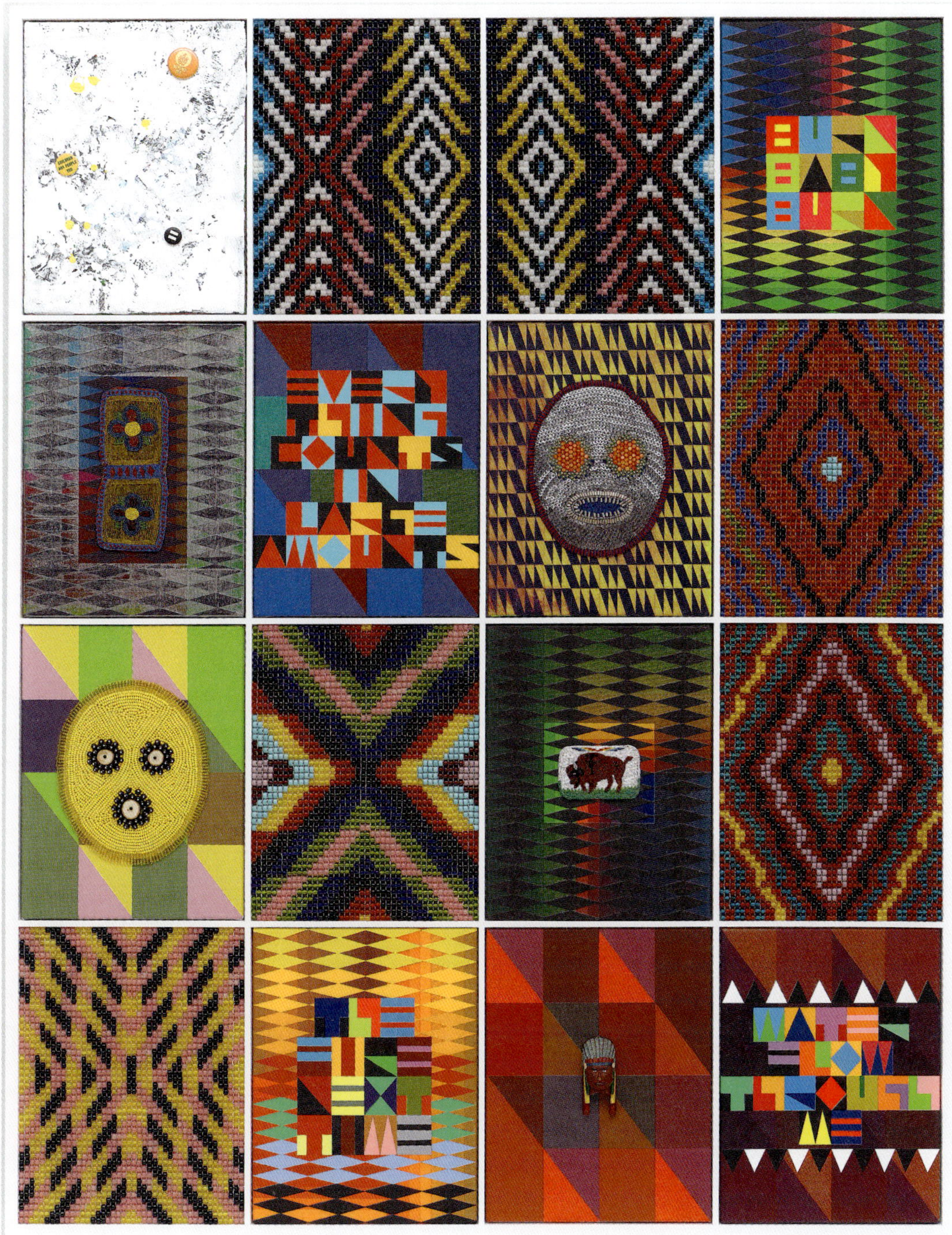

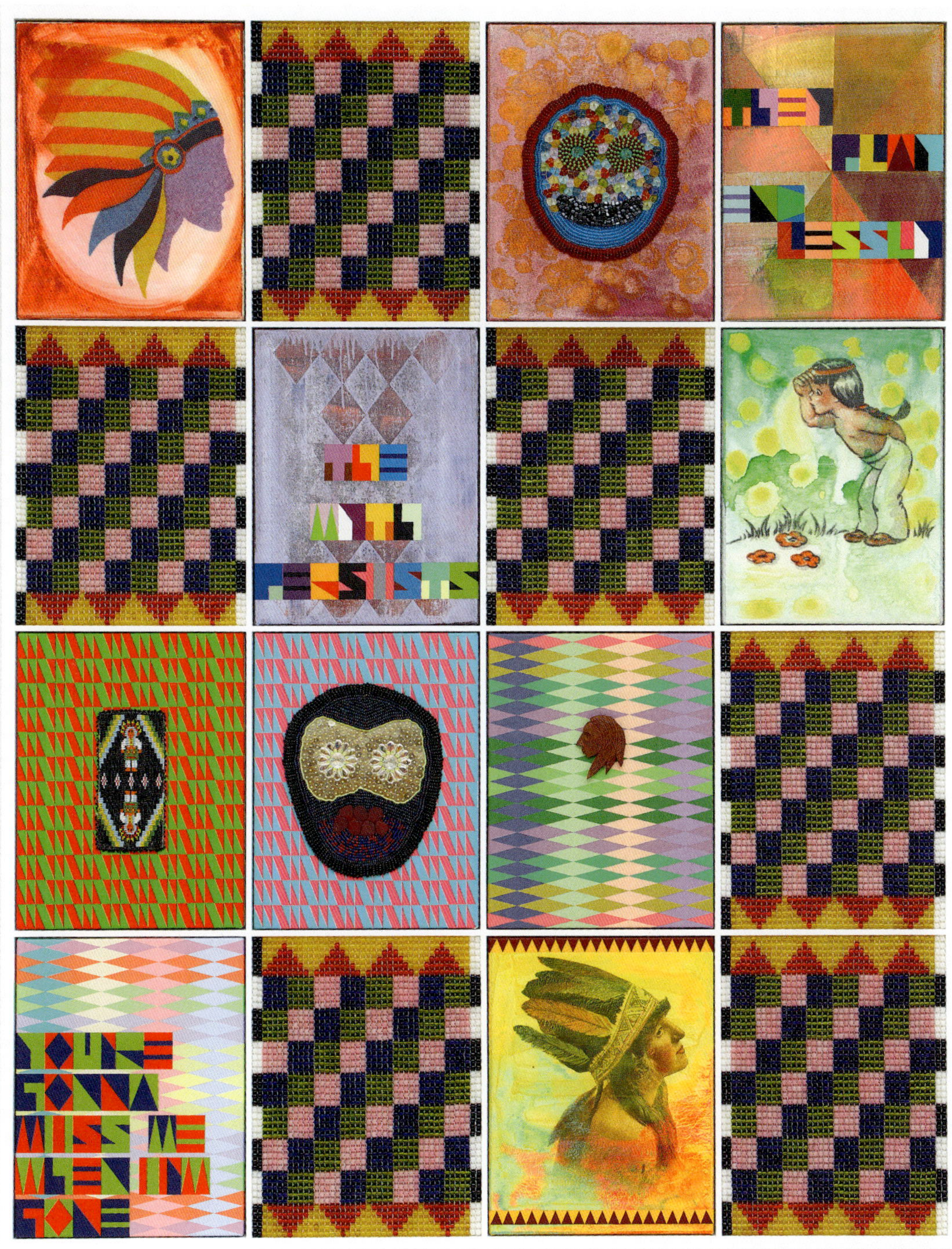

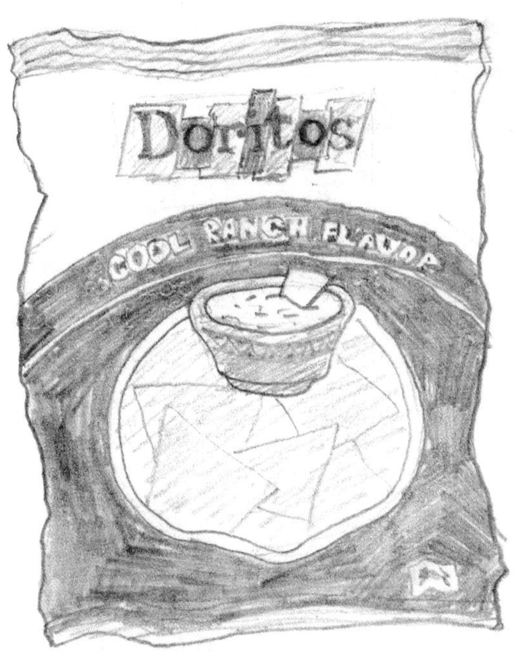
Doritos
COOL RANCH FLAVOR

181109

Field No.

—

Neg. No.

Acc. 3784

 2-21

Provenience: Toksook Bay, Nelson Is., Alaska

People or Culture: Yupik Eskimo

Object: tortilla chips

Material: —

Description: "Doritos" cool ranch flavor
(1 packet - 1-1/8 oz.)

Used as gift in seal party.

Dimensions: —
(in cm.)

Collection: Dr. Ann Fienup-Riordan

*Sweet Bitter Love: An Initiative of
Toward Common Cause* ●

The Newberry Library
May 28, 2021–September 18, 2021

Installation views:
pp. 30–39

Beyond the Horizon ■

Kavi Gupta Gallery
November 13, 2021–January 8, 2022

Installation views:
pp. 90–101

Elbridge Ayer (E. A.) Burbank
American, 1858–1949

Boneta
Fort Sill, Oklahoma Territory,
undated [1897]
Oil on canvas
21 1/8 x 14 1/4 inches (53.6 x 36.1 cm)
Vault oversize Ayer Art Burbank,
No. 73
Newberry Library, Chicago
● pp. 14, 43

Chief American Horse
Lame Deer, Montana, 1897
Oil on canvas
13 3/4 x 9 7/8 inches (33 x 25 cm)
Vault oversize Ayer Art Burbank,
No. 72
Newberry Library, Chicago
● p. 45

Chief Joseph
[Nespelem, Washington], 1897
Oil on panel
8 3/4 x 6 5/8 inches (22.2 x 16.8 cm)
Vault oversize Ayer Art Burbank,
No. 74
Newberry Library, Chicago
● p. 47

Chief Pretty Eagle
St. Xavier, Montana, 1897
Oil on canvas
21 1/8 x 14 1/4 inches (53.6 x 36.1 cm)
Vault oversize Ayer Art Burbank,
No. 58
Newberry Library, Chicago
● p. 49

Geronimo
Fort Sill, Oklahoma Territory,
undated [1897]
Oil on board
8 3/4 x 6 ¾ inches (22.2 x 17.1 cm)
Vault oversize Ayer Art Burbank,
No. 80
Newberry Library, Chicago
● p. 51

Gi-aum-e Hon-o-me-tah
Fort Sill, Oklahoma Territory,
undated [1897]
Oil on panel
8 3/4 x 6 5/8 inches (22.2 x 17.4 cm)
Vault oversize Ayer Art Burbank,
No. 77
Newberry Library, Chicago
● p. 53

Chief Po-Ka-Gon, Pottawattomie
Lee, Michigan, 1898
Oil on canvas
14 1/4 x 10 1/4 inches (36.1 x 26 cm)
Vault oversize Ayer Art Burbank,
No. 54
Newberry Library, Chicago
● p. 55

Hawgone
Fort Sill, Oklahoma Territory,
undated [1898]
Oil on panel
21 1/8 x 14 1/4 inches (51 x 31 cm)
Vault oversize Ayer Art Burbank,
No. 57
Newberry Library, Chicago
● p. 57

Pahl-Lee
Keams Canyon, Arizona, 1898
Oil on panel
8 5/8 x 6 5/8 inches (22 x 17 cm)
Vault oversize Ayer Art Burbank,
No. 60
Newberry Library, Chicago
● p. 59

Chief Red Cloud
Pine Ridge, South Dakota, 1899
Oil on canvas
14 1/8 x 10 1/4 inches (35.8 x 26 cm)
Vault oversize Ayer Art Burbank,
No. 66.
Newberry Library, Chicago
● p. 61

Chief Keokuk
Sac & Fox Agency, Oklahoma
Territory, 1900
Oil on canvas
13 7/8 x 9 7/8 inches (35.2 x 25 cm)
Vault oversize Ayer Art Burbank,
No. 64
Newberry Library, Chicago
● p. 63

Chief Wolf-Robe
Darlington, Oklahoma Territory, 1901
Oil on canvas
13 3/4 x 9 7/8 inches (33 x 25 cm)
Vault oversize Ayer Art Burbank,
No. 67
Newberry Library, Chicago
● p. 65

Field Museum Catalogue Cards,
Accession 3784, Nelson Island Seal
Party Collection
1990
Printed and typewritten text (recto),
graphite drawing on paper (verso)
3 x 5 inches (7.6 x 12.7 cm)
The Field Museum, Chicago

Card 181107, *Soda Pop*.
"'Diet Pepsi' (1 can – 12 oz.)."
● p. 116–17

Card 181108, *Crackers*.
"A) 'Royal Kreem' pilot crackers (1
pkg. – 14 ½ oz.) B) large, round soda
crackers (6)."
● p. 73

Card 181109, *Tortilla Chips*.
"'Doritos' cool ranch flavor (1 packet
– 1 1/8 oz.)."
● pp. 174–75

Card 181110, *"Instant Lunch"*.
"'Maruchan' oriental noodles with
vegetables and egg, beef."
● pp. 4–5

Card 181111, *Candy*.
"A) 'Whoopers' malted milk candy (1
packet – 3/4 oz.), B) 'Switzer' cherry
licorice (1 pkg. – 0.8 oz.), C) 'Tootsie
Roll' orange pop (1 – 0.6 oz.), and D)
'Sugar Daddy" caramel pop (1)."
● p. 20

Card 181112, *Tea Bags*.
"Red Rose" (11)."
●

Card 181113, *Soap*.
"A) 'Ivory' (1 bar - 3 1/2 oz.), B)
'Irish Spring' (1 bar – 2.5 oz.)."
● pp. 10–11

Card 181114, *Toothbrush*.
"'Oral B', youth size, clear handle."
●

Card 181115, *Matches*.
"'Diamond' – Mother's Day (1 book),
The Airplane (1 book), and The Box
Camera (2 books)."
● pp. 102–103

Card 181116, *Snuff*.
"Copenhagen (1 tin – 1.2 oz.)."
● pp. 40–41

Card 181117, *Work Gloves*.
"Boss", white, boys size (1 pair).
Used as gift in seal party."
●

Card 181118, *Disposable Diapers*.
"Decorated waistband (2)."
● pp. 28–29

Card 181119, *Toilet Paper*.
"White (1 roll)."
● pp. 88–89

Card 181120, *Soap Dish*.
"'Pretty Neat,' red."
● pp. 132–33

Card 181121, *Cloth*.
"Cotton, rectangular lengths – multi
colored floral (2), blue & white
checked (1), gold flowered on
blue (1)."
● pp. 66–67

Card 181122, *Yarn*.
"Red (6 strands), white (3 strands),
and multi colored (3 strands)."
●

Mississippi Band of Choctaw,
Cherokee, born 1972

Acc. 3784, 2021
Digitally printed wallpaper on vinyl
Dimensions variable
Courtesy of Jeffrey Gibson
●■ endpapers, p. 25

Boneta, Comanche, 2021
Cotton rag paper, archival pigment
print, glass beads, nylon thread,
vintage beaded belt (glass beads,
suede, and cotton thread), vintage
beaded barrettes (glass beads,
suede, polyester, and thread),
vintage ring toss game from Japan
(print, cardboard, and clear plastic),
brass repoussé, vintage papers, glass
beads, urethane, and acrylic paint
60 1/2 × 44 inches (153.7 × 111.8 cm)
Collection of Mitchell
and Debbie Rechler
●■ pp. 23, 135, 137 (detail)

Chief Black Coyote, 2021
Cotton rag paper, vintage beaded
barrette (glass beads, polyester,
and suede cotton thread), vintage
beaded belt buckle (glass beads,
suede, polyester, and thread),
vintage pin, beaded belt (glass
beads, cotton thread), glass beads,
nylon thread, vintage papers, glass
beads, urethane, and acrylic paint
67 1/2 x 44 inches (171.5 x 111.8 cm)
Collection of Schuyler and Jon Levin
●■ pp. 139, 141 (detail)

Chief Pretty Eagle, 2021
Cotton rag paper, inkjet print,
vintage beaded eyeglass case (glass
beads, polyester, thread, suede),
vintage beaded barrette (glass beads,
polyester, and thread), vintage
papers, found pin, glass beads,
glitter, urethane, and acrylic paint
60 3/8 x 44 inches (153.4 x 111.8 cm)
Collection of Mitchell
and Debbie Rechler
●■ pp. 143, 145 (detail)

Christian Naiche, 2021
Cotton rag paper, vintage beaded
picture frame (glass beads, cotton
fabric, cardboard, velvet, cotton
thread, and suede), vintage pin,
vintage beaded barrette (glass
beads, suede, polyester, and thread),
vintage beaded belt buckle (glass
beads, suede, polyester, and thread),
vintage beaded whimsey (glass
beads, velvet, cardboard, saw dust,
and thread), glass beads, nylon
thread, vintage papers, glass beads,
urethane, and acrylic paint
67 1/2 x 44 inches (171.5 x 111.8 cm)
Collection of The Andrew W. Mellon
Foundation
●■ pp. 147, 149 (detail)

Pahl-Lee, 2021
Cotton rag paper, archival pigment
print, vintage beaded handbag
(glass beads, cotton fabric, leather,
brass enclosure, polyester, and
cotton thread), glass beads, vintage
papers, glass beads, urethane, and
acrylic paint
60 1/2 x 44 inches (153.7 x 111.8 cm)
Collection of Jill and Nick Woodman
●■ pp. 151, 153 (detail)

White Swan, 2021
Cotton rag paper, archival pigment
print, vintage beaded barrette
(glass beads, suede, and cotton
thread), vintage beaded appliqué
(glass beads, polyester, and thread),
glass beads, nylon thread, vintage
papers, glass beads, urethane, and
acrylic paint
60 1/2 x 44 inches (153.7 x 111.8 cm)
Collection of Arnie
and Elizabeth Lizan
●■ pp. 155, 157 (detail)

Black Beauty, 2021
Glass beads, acrylic felt,
polyester fiber fill, artificial sinew,
nylon thread, and vintage beaded
elements (glass beads, suede, and
cotton thread)
16 x 23 x 13 1/4 inches (40.6 x 58.4 x
33.7 cm)
Collection of Barbara Goldfarb
■ p. 159

BY ANY MEANS NECESSARY, 2021
Canvas, acrylic paint, glass beads,
artificial sinew, nylon thread,
vintage beaded belt buckle
(suede, glass beads, and cotton
thread), vintage beaded whimsey
(cotton fabric, velvet, glass beads,
and cotton thread), and vintage
beaded bag (suede, glass beads,
and cotton thread)
66 1/2 x 50 1/2 x 3 1/4 inches (168.9 x
128.3 x 8.3 cm)
Collection of Rose Art Museum,
Brandeis University. Edward and
Bertha Rose Acquisition Fund and
Mortimer and Sara Hays Acquisition
Fund, 2022.8
■ pp. 161

Firebelly, 2021
Glass beads, acrylic felt, polyester
fiber fill, artificial sinew, nylon thread,
and vintage beaded elements (glass
beads, suede, and cotton thread)
16 x 23 x 13 1/4 inches (40.6 x 58.4 x
33.7 cm)
Collection of Sundeep
and Trista Mullangi
■ p. 163

I'M LOOKING FOR SUNSHINE, 2021
Canvas, acrylic paint, glass beads,
artificial sinew, nylon thread,
wooden beads, vinyl beads, sea
glass beads, vintage beaded coin
purse (suede, glass beads, and
cotton thread), and vintage beaded
tie (glass beads, cotton fabric, and
cotton thread)
66 1/2 x 50 1/2 x 3 1/4 inches (168.9 x
128.3 x 8.3 cm)
Private collection, Europe
■ p. 165

MAKE ME FEEL IT, 2021
Canvas, acrylic paint, vintage beaded
barrette, glass beads, artificial sinew,
tumbled stone beads, plastic beads,
wooden beads, cross pearl pendants,
and nylon thread
66 1/2 x 50 1/2 x 3 1/4 inches (168.9 x
128.3 x 8.3 cm)
Collection of OZ Art, Bentonville,
Arkansas
■ p. 167

OVER THE RAINBOW, 2021
Canvas, acrylic paint, vintage beaded
necktie, archival pigment print on
rice paper, glass beads, artificial
sinew, wooden beads, vinyl sequins,
brass adornment, druzy bead, and
nylon thread
66 1/2 x 50 1/2 x 3 1/4 inches (168.9 x
128.3 x 8.3 cm)
Collection of Carl & Marilynn Thoma
Foundation
■ p. 169

THE FIRE NEXT TIME, 2021
Canvas, acrylic paint, glass beads,
artificial sinew, nylon thread, vintage
beaded belt buckle (suede, glass
beads, and cotton thread), vintage
beaded wallet (glass beads, cotton
fabric, and cotton thread), and
vintage wood tie slide
66 1/2 x 50 1/2 x 3 1/4 inches (168.9 x
128.3 x 8.3 cm)
Collection of Craig Hartzman
and James John
■ p. 171

THEY PLAY ENDLESSLY, 2021
Canvas, acrylic paint, vintage beaded
wallet, vintage wooden broach,
archival pigment print on rice paper,
glass beads, artificial sinew, hematite
beads, plastic beads, druzy beads,
metal sequins, turquoise beads, and
nylon thread
66 1/2 x 50 1/2 x 3 1/4 inches (168.9 x
128.3 x 8.3 cm)
Private collection, San Francisco
■ pp. 173

Pages 4–5; 10–11; 20 fig. 3;
28–29; 40–41; 66–67; 72 (fig. 2);
73 (figs. 3a, 3b); 88–89; 102–103;
116–17; 132–33; 174–75:
Photographer John M. Kelly
© The Field Museum, Image No.
181111CC, Cat. No. 181111.

Pages 23 (fig. 4); 96–97; 135;
137 (detail); 139; 141 (detail); 143;
145 (detail); 147, 148–149 (detail); 151;
153 (detail); 155; 157 (detail), 159; 161;
163; 165; 167; 169; 171; and 173:
Photos by Max Yawney.

Pages 31–39:
Photos by Nathan Keay.

Page 70 (fig. 1):
Produced by VAM Studios.

Page 79 (fig. 4):
Photo courtesy of the John D.
and Catherine T. MacArthur
Foundation, 2007.

Pages 81 (fig. 5); 91–95; 98–101;
106 (fig. 1); 111 (fig. 2); 143; and
145 (detail):
Photos by John Lusis.

Page 82 (fig. 6):
Photo by Brian Barlow.

Page 130 (fig. 6):
Photo by Tatyana Tenebaum
and Megan Stahl.

This publication was produced by the Smart Museum of Art, The University of Chicago, to commemorate Jeffrey Gibson's exhibitions *Sweet Bitter Love: An Initiative of Toward Common Cause* (May 28–September 18, 2021), at the Newberry Library, Chicago, and *Beyond the Horizon* (November 13, 2021–January 8, 2022), at Kavi Gupta, Chicago.

Sweet Bitter Love: An Initiative of Toward Common Cause was a collaboration between the Smart Museum of Art at the University of Chicago and the Newberry Library. It was an initiative of *Toward Common Cause: Art, Social Change, and the MacArthur Fellows Program at 40*, which was organized by the Smart Museum of Art in collaboration with exhibition, programmatic, and research partners across Chicago. *Toward Common Cause* was supported by the John D. and Catherine T. MacArthur Foundation and curated by Abigail Winograd, MacArthur Fellows Program Fortieth Anniversary Exhibition Curator, Smart Museum of Art, The University of Chicago.

Support for the catalogue was provided by Kavi Gupta, Chicago.

Kavi Gupta

ISBN: 9780935573657

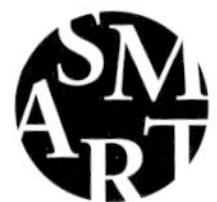

Smart Museum of Art
The University of Chicago
5550 S. Greenwood Avenue
Chicago, Illinois 60637
773.702.0200
smartmuseum.uchicago.edu

Publication Manager:
Gail Ana Gomez

Copy Editor:
Amy Teschner

Image and Research Assistants:
Brian Barlow
Norman Mora Quintero

Design and Production:
Unyimeabasi Udoh

Printing and Binding:
Balto Print, Vilnius, Lithuania

All works by Jeffrey Gibson are © Jeffrey Gibson.

Library of Congress Control Number: 2022938362

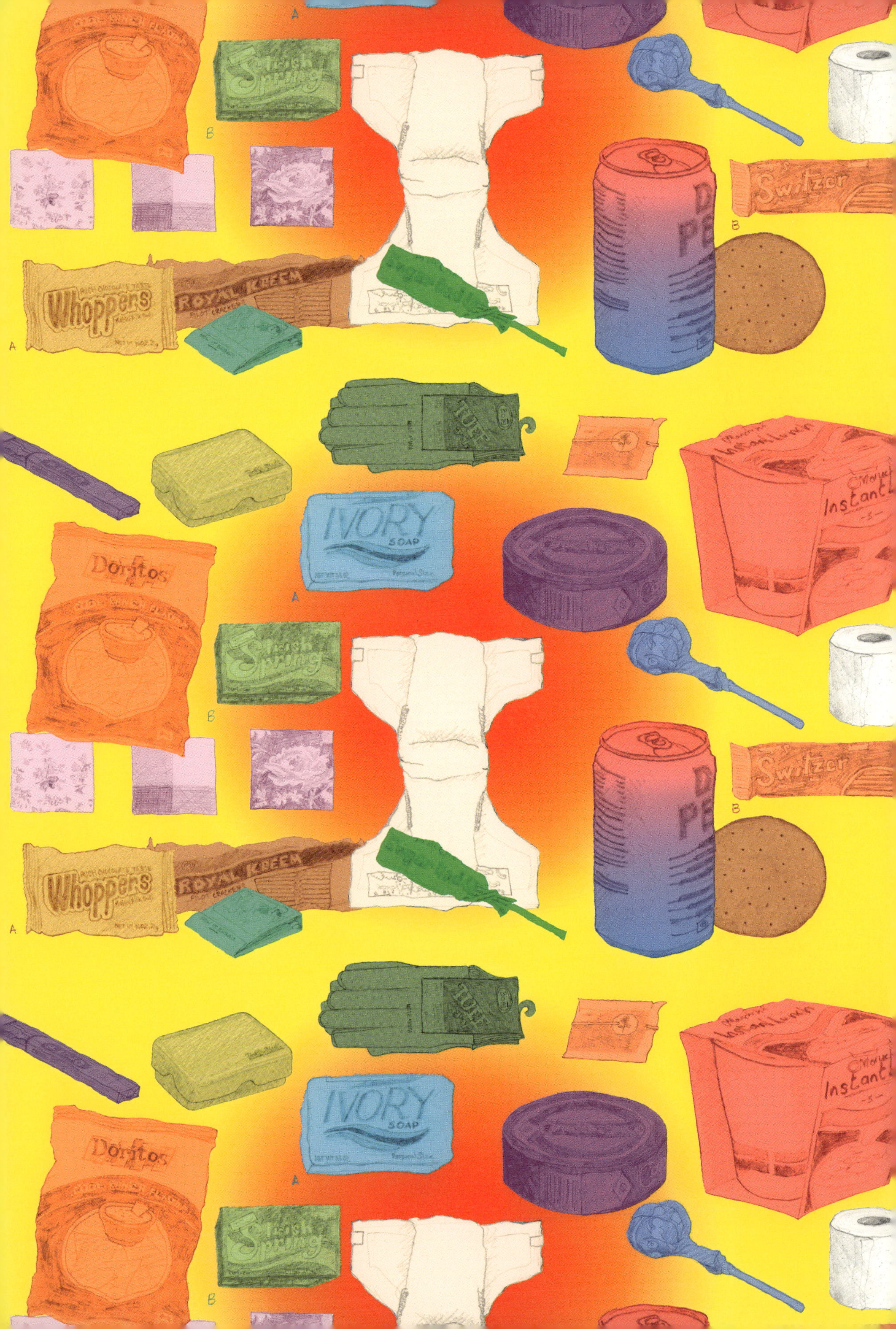
Spring
Whoppers
RICH CHOCOLATE TASTE
ROYAL KREEM
PILOT CRACKERS
Switzer
TUFF
Doritos
IVORY
SOAP
Instant